Lies
PEOPLE
TELL

An FBI Agent's toolkit for catching
liars and cheats.

Frank Runles

© Frank Runles 2021

ISBN: 978-1-66781-089-8

eBook ISBN: 978-1-66781-090-4

Dedication

For my wife, Karrie. Thanks for believing. You're my rock and I love you.

For my daughter, Natali. You are the love of my life and keep me young.

For my friend, Lisa Barber. Thanks for giving me the inspiration for this book.

TABLE OF CONTENTS

INTRODUCTION

You ever have that feeling you are being lied to? That the person you are talking to is not being honest with you? Maybe you can't quite put your finger on it, but a little voice tells you something is not quite right.

Listen to that voice, because it is telling you something important.

The amygdala is the oldest part of the human brain, and it tells us when there is danger nearby. It is the part of the brain that governs your senses and allows you to react to danger and threats.

In the distant past of human evolution, the amygdala played a much larger part of everyday life. The caveman may not have seen the saber-tooth tiger lying in wait in the tall grass, but the amygdala sent him a signal, whether through scent, sight, or sound, that there was danger nearby and he went on high alert.

But with the advance of civilization and society, we don't listen to our amygdalae anymore. We blithely (and incorrectly) believe we are safe or that we already know the dangers around us.

We may not have to watch out for saber-tooth tigers today, but, believe me, predators are stalking unsuspecting people all the time.

Deceit and playing fast and loose with the truth have become accepted in modern society. With the rise of technology and in the age of information overload, we have been lied to and deceived so frequently that we, as a society, have become immune to it.

Our political leaders deceive us with slick double talk. We are fed a steady stream of disinformation and fake news. Slick salespeople hook us into buying things we don't need or don't deliver as promised. It is so prevalent that we don't even notice it anymore. We just shrug our collective shoulders and say, "It's just the way it is."

It Doesn't Have to Be This Way

Unchecked and undetected deception can have many negative effects on our lives and on our family's well-being.

Have you ever said to yourself, *If I had known what I know now, I wouldn't have done that*, or *I can't believe I fell for that load of BS!* I have. We all have.

When we are deceived, we can lose our money and lessen our power to provide for and protect our family.

Our status in our community can be compromised and our self-worth diminished.

When we realize we've been duped, we're angry! We want vengeance. We want to get back at the villain. Unfortunately, that almost never happens, and we are left feeling defeated and betrayed by the world.

It's just wrong.

The Genesis of This Book

When I was new FBI agent, my first assignment was Buffalo, New York. For some unknown reason, in the 1990s, Buffalo, New York, was a hotbed for telemarketers with numerous telemarketing boiler rooms operating in the Buffalo area. The problem was significant enough that the Buffalo FBI office started a telemarketing task force to address the problem to which I was assigned.

Once assigned to the task force, I started an investigation of a telemarketing group operating out of a boiler room on Delaware Avenue that specifically targeted senior citizens who had been previously scammed by other telemarketers. They called themselves WNY Recovery Inc. WNY Recovery Inc guaranteed their victims they would recover all of the senior citizen's previously lost money for a small ten percent fee, paid up front, of course.

In the world of telemarketing, lists of people who are having financial problems or who have recently won or inherited large amounts of money are bought and sold. Even more nefarious, lists of prior telemarketing victims are also bought and sold. These victims have already shown a penchant for falling for the slick talk of a telemarketer. They are like pre-approved victims.

I know people will say, "Hey, if you're dumb enough to fall for this once or, even worse, twice well, too bad for you." But consider how easily your mom, dad, grandfather, or grandmother could be victimized by a slick fraudster.

I spent weeks calling and interviewing these victims. Most were very reluctant to admit that they had been defrauded a second time. Many had never told anyone that they had been defrauded the first time. There was a lot of shame and embarrassment.

This is where I started to really learn how to interview people. I had to gently coax the truth out of the victims using the few interviewing tools I possessed at that time in my career.

After interviewing these victims, it was clear that they were very trusting people and totally clueless when it came to be being deceived. It was heartbreaking to hear their stories of how they lost their meager savings and how it had destroyed their financial security.

I'm telling you, when you hear a eighty-year-old woman sobbing on the phone telling you how she trusted the "nice young man" when he promised to get her money back, it changes you. Thinking back on it still makes me angry.

I learned a few things during this investigation.

One, I have a knack for interviewing people and getting them to open up to me. This was probably my greatest asset as an FBI agent. If an agent can't talk to people, they are ineffective (and probably will end up in FBI management!).

Two, because people aren't informed, they are easily fooled.

Three, to be a better investigator, I needed to learn as much as I could about detecting deception.

I spent the rest of my FBI career learning and researching how to effectively detect deception. I became a better interviewer and investigator because of what I had learned. So, after all these years, I decided to write this book to share what I have learned over my 20 year FBI career.

I never want to see someone's future stolen because they don't know what I know. After decades of protecting the American public, I feel obligated to share what I have learned through years of experience, training, and research in the area of deception.

My hope is that after you have finished this book, you will listen to what people say in a different way. You will read things in a different light. For lack of a better term, your BS meter will be pegged out!

If you practice what I will teach you in the following pages, I promise the following:

1. You will recognize when someone is trying to deceive you.
2. You will become a better communicator.
3. You will understand people better.
4. You will be better armed to protect your family and your money.
5. You will become more successful.

This book is not an academic tome. It is meant to be a common sense, easy-to-read, and, hopefully, entertaining guide that helps you recognize the various ways people try to deceive us every day. That is not to say what I teach isn't backed up by research. It most definitely is. The lessons in this book are drawn from research done by such esteemed researchers as Susan H. Adams and John P. Jarvis (2006), Judee Burgoon and Tiantian Qin (2006), Stephen Porter and John Yuille (1996), Don Rabon (1996), Avinoam Sapir (1987), Wendell "Buddy" Rudacille (1994), and many others.

What I teach is meant to be portable and practical. Portable and practical in that you can take the knowledge learned with you and easily use it in your everyday life, both personal and professional. I want you to be able to listen to what you hear and automatically know someone is using deceptive language.

The book is broken into two sections.

The first section covers indicators of deception. These are the broad strokes of clues I look for in deceptive language.

In chapters one through eight, I teach how to use Deceptive Language Analysis (DLA) to analyze statements (both verbal and written) and how to formulate an interview strategy to get to the truth. You will learn how to detect deception and gain insight into the motivations and behaviors of people.

We delve into listening and why we have such a hard time doing it. We discuss how to determine whether a statement is balanced or out of balance. I show you how to recognize unique sensory details, spatial details, and where emotions should show up in statements. I also explain how extraneous information is used to deceive, how time can tell you when someone is being deceptive, and how to differentiates between appropriate equivocations and inappropriate equivocations based on the statement's context.

In the second section, we get into the nitty gritty of the specific parts of language used to deceive.

Chapters nine through thirteen explain the significance of the cast of characters found in statements, how pronouns tell us what and who is important to someone, the many ways verbs can be used to deceive, how intensifiers and minimizers are used to convince but not convey information, and how time jumps are employed to move a story along and skip over the uncomfortable parts. We finish with how to formulate amplification questions to extract more information from the people trying to fool us.

Throughout this book, I use statements from criminal investigations I was personally involved in and ones I've gathered over the years while consulting with law enforcement agencies across the United States on their cases.

Some of these cases and statements will be familiar (Casey Anthony, George Zimmerman, Susan Smith, Jerry Sandusky, and Oscar Pretorius) and some less well known. I use these as illustrations of deceptive language because they are good examples of the points I make and also because they are just interesting stories. It gives the reader a chance to go behind the scenes of the crimes, so to speak. But I also give examples of how these deceptive language tricks can be used in business and in interpersonal interactions. This book is intended to arm you, the average citizen, with the tools to catch liars before you get fooled.

If you're ready, let's get started!

SECTION ONE:

Indicators of Veracity

CHAPTER 1:

The Difference between Lies and Deception

After spending more than twenty years as an FBI Special Agent interviewing thousands of people, I've learned a few things. One, lying is stressful and hard for most people to do. Two, being deceptive is much easier than telling a lie. Three, people always do what's easiest for them.

During my FBI career, I interviewed a lot of different characters: white collar criminals embezzling money and running fraud schemes, corrupt politicians, Russian gangsters, union organizers cracking heads, Organized Crime figures, kidnappers, jihadists in Iraq and Guantanamo Bay, gang bangers selling dope, members of biker gangs, sexual predators, reluctant witnesses and the victims of crimes.

The one thing they all had in common: They all used deceptive language, but they avoided telling outright lies because the act of lying is hard to do.

Lying is stressful. Coming up with a plausible story on the fly is difficult, and keeping the facts straight so your lie is consistent is a mental challenge.

No one wants to be caught in a lie. That's why we use deceptive language instead.

You may ask what's the difference between deception and a lie. Deception is when one uses certain linguistic techniques to leave someone with a false impression or belief. A lie is more complicated and comes in two forms: lies by commission and lies by omission.

Lies by commission are fabricated stories. The person who lies by commission must come up with an untruthful story with sufficient detail to make it appear truthful, yet not enough detail where they can be later tripped up by some astute interviewer. I call this The Lie.

Lies by omission occur when the person just doesn't answer the question or leaves out pertinent details to a story so as not to entrap themselves. They do a lot of talking without ever telling you anything pertinent or relevant to the issue at hand. Lies by omission are, by nature, deceptive language.

People use deceptive language for a variety of reasons. They don't want to get locked into a story that can be easily disproved. They may be trying to hide illegal behavior. They use deceptive language because the information being sought is embarrassing or they are trying to protect themselves or someone else. There are unlimited reasons why people use deceptive language.

Many times, when asked a direct question concerning some nefarious act, people will give a deceptive answer but not lie outright. They will say things like "I don't remember" (negation, equivocation, lack of memory versus lack of knowledge); "I wouldn't do something like that" (negation, equivocation); "I would never do something like that" (intensifier, negation, equivocation); "Why would I do something like that?" (asking you to answer your own question). They will provide an abundance of unimportant information while not answering the question (extraneous information), and provide little verifiable detail (lacking unique sensory and spatial detail).

These are just a few of the linguistic tricks people use to deceive.

Although I had extensive experience interviewing and interrogating people in my FBI career, there were times when I struggled to articulate how I knew someone was being untruthful. My experience and common sense told me I was getting a load of BS, but I didn't really know why I knew this. I just knew.

As a professional investigator, that's a quandary.

Today, I believe that a lot of other people are in the same quandary as I was.

People know when they are being lied to, but they usually don't know why they know it. In my case, once I knew what to look for I could very easily pick up on deceptive language. Not The Lie, just deceptive language. When you are looking for The Lie, you stop listening to what is really being said to you.

Take, for example, the following excerpts from an interview of Timothy McVeigh, the Oklahoma City Bomber.

Timothy McVeigh statements to Newsweek, July 3, 1995

Newsweek: **This is the question that everyone wants to know – did you do it?**

McVeigh: **The only way we can really answer that is that we are going to plead not guilty.**

Jones (McVeigh's attorney): **And we're going to go to trial.**

Newsweek: **But you've got a chance right now to say, "hell no!"**

McVeigh: **We can't do that.**

You see, even McVeigh had a hard time lying. He could have very easily said, "I didn't do it. I'm innocent." But he didn't. Instead, he said, "We are going to plead not guilty." Even when given the chance to say he didn't do the bombing, he can't tell that lie.

How about a more contemporary example? The following is a transcript from an interview of Charlie Sheen by Piers Morgan.

Charlie Sheen has never hit a woman

Piers: **Charlie, there have been reports in the papers over the last few years, hinting at violence by you towards... one was towards your wife, and one was towards a porn star in a hotel... Were they true?**

Did the drugs make you violent? Do you regret what happened on those two instances?

Charlie: Now, those are two instances where the scoreboard does not lie… The Aspen thing was thrown out. The judge was like get this guy out of my County, I'm basically depressed with him... And then the police report in New York didn't reflect anything, and those are the guys who are going to report the facts…their jobs are on the line, so I just offer people those.

(0:32) Piers: Have you ever hit a woman?

Charlie: Uh, I have not, no, no. Women are not to be hit. They are to be hugged and caressed, you know.

Piers: A few people who are very close to you have expressed real concern…

(0:44) *Charlie:* (interrupting) I'm sorry. There was an incident years ago and everybody thought I hit her. I was trying to, uh, contain her and I had her arms and we both went to the ground and she hit her...

Piers: Who was that?

Charlie: Her initials are B.A. I'll give you that much. Um, I don't want to make the whole thing about her, you know. And I, I, felt terrible and I delivered her to the plastic surgeon and tried to like, you know. And everybody said you hit her, and I'm like no, she hit her thing and I felt bad about that…whatever, it's all over…

Piers: And do you…reg…?

(1:07) *Charlie:* And I felt bad about that one, yeah.

Piers: And you regret that?

Charlie: Yeah, she was attacking me though, with a, with a small fork, like a cocktail fork…and I think she had it with her. That's the weird part. What was she doing with, like a, shrimp fork in her purse?

Piers: But is there ever any…?

Charlie: She stole it, clearly, from a buffet…Sorry…

Piers: But is there every any defense…?

Charlie: Well, you can't…whatever story you come up with…it sounds like you made it up. And that's the truth. And that's what happened.

Piers: But you regret that incident?

Charlie: Oh, God, yeah, yeah. But I never really told the story about that, because everybody was under a gag order or something. But there were heinous things that led up to that, that I was trying to fend off… Whatever. I'll own it. So, I just remembered that when you asked, that's the only time and it was presumed that I had done so.

Charlie denied hitting a woman, and then couldn't help himself and admitted that he did, in fact, hit a woman. He used extraneous information to justify his actions, but he still couldn't bring himself to stick with the lie. Lying is hard.

The Ability to Detect Deception

Opinions vary on people's ability to detect deception. If you look on the Internet, you'll find that there are many reports and studies declaring that a person's accuracy level at detecting lies ranges from forty to sixty percent. After reviewing many of these reports and studies I don't disagree with their findings, but I believe their findings are skewed to the negative due to the methodology used in the studies. Let me explain.

Most of the studies have two major shortcomings. They rely too heavily on body language to detect deception and the subjects used in the studies face no consequences if they are caught lying.

Most of the academic studies done in the area of deception detection use students as test subjects. The students face no serious consequences if caught in a lie. Their lack of "skin in the game" emboldens them to lie and greatly lessens the fear of being caught in a lie. If you are not afraid of getting caught, you will be more relaxed and appear more believable. A college student in an academic study, no matter how scrupulously the tests are conducted, has a different mindset than someone who has embezzled money from his company and is questioned about the missing money. This person has "skin in the game". Their anxiety is real. They could lose their job, be imprisoned, heavily fined, damage their reputation in the community, and possibly lose their family. Many bad thing can and probably will happen when this person's crime is uncovered.

On the other hand, the student posing as someone who embezzled money from a company has none of these concerns. The student's anxiety level is low. What negative consequences does the student face, after all, if the interviewer accurately detects deception? Because of the lack of true stress, the student's behavior is vastly different than an actual person trying to deceive someone.

The other problem with the studies is that they rely too much on interpreting body language as a means of detecting deception.

In the July 2018 edition of *Psychology Today*, Joe Navarro, author of the book *What Every Body is Saying*, posited that the over-reliance on body language as being good indicators of deceptive behavior is wrongheaded. Navarro wrote, "It is time to stop teaching and preaching that we can detect deception through nonverbals and teach what we can use nonverbals for. What is it? That we humans transmit through our body language, what we think, feel, desire, and fear; and that we communicate this effectively in real time. That when we are stressed, bothered, disappointed, disturbed, anxious, worried, concerned, uncertain, exasperated, or mad, our bodies reveal that information nonverbally by any number of expressions throughout the body, including through the use of pacifiers or what Paul Ekman calls 'adaptive behaviors'". In essence we, all of us, can be 'issue detectors' as I often say in my lectures, but that is all. That's all we can say, that something is wrong or not right—that there is an issue—but no more."

The reality is that there are no unique physical behaviors associated with deception or truthfulness. As interviewers, however, we can sway a person's reaction to the questioning. If we question someone aggressively, whether they are innocent or guilty, anxious and defensive behaviors will be exhibited. The guilty because they fear being caught and punished; the innocent because they fear they won't be believed and wrongfully punished. This is why we have to be mindful not to let our biases dictate our behavior.

In his book, *Duped: Truth-Default Theory and the Social Science of Lying and Deception* (University of Alabama Press, Tuscaloosa, AL, 2020), author Timothy R. Levine explains his extensive research in the area of the detection of deception. Based on his research, Levine came up with the Truth Default Theory (TDT), which posits that most people possess the truth default that "involves a passive presumption of honesty due to a failure to actively consider the possibility of deceit at all or as a fallback cognitive state after a failure to obtain sufficient affirmative evidence for deception." In other words, most people naturally believe other people, especially when there is no obvious evidence indicating dishonesty. According to Levine, most people have a truth bias, which "is the tendency to believe that another person's communication is honest independent of actual honesty."

I don't disagree with Levine's opinion. Most people want to believe others are honest and are not trying to deceive them. We want to give people the benefit of the doubt, even when the voice in our head tells us to be wary. It is especially hard to believe a friend or relative may be deceptive. This is why so many families refuse to believe that those close to them are untruthful. It is easier to refuse to acknowledge the obvious truth than to believe that they are deceptive.

As a professional law enforcement office, my truth default is pretty much non-existent. I've been lied to far too often and seen too much of the human condition to automatically believe what I hear. Cynical? Yes, but I temper it with the knowledge that people are deceptive for many reasons, and not all of them are nefarious. Many times, people are deceptive because they have done something stupid and are embarrassed. Other times they are trying to protect themselves, their families, or their reputations. They are being deceptive, but not necessarily trying to harm others.

Researcher Charlie Bond conducted two of the largest research studies ever done examining what behavioral cues people associate with deception. (The Global Research Team, "A World of Lies", *Journal of Cross Cultural Psychology*, 37, no 1, (January 2006): 60-74) Bond collected data from 75 countries in 43 different languages.

In Bond's first study, 20 males and 20 females from 58 different countries were asked, "How can you tell when people are lying?" The most frequent answer was that a liar will not look you in the eyes (gaze aversion); 63.7% of respondents gave that answer. The second most common answer was nervousness coming in at 28%.

In a second study, 40 subjects from 63 countries were given a list of behavioral cues which may indicate deception and was asked to select which cues most likely indicate deception. A whopping 71.5% picked gaze aversion as the most likely indicator of deception and nervous behavior as the second most at 66%.

But when the question was changed from" How do you know when you are being lied to?" to something like "Recall a time when you learned you were lied to, how did you discover the lie?" The answers shifted from non-verbal behavioral cues to verbal cues such as inconsistent information and talking to much (extraneous information, trying to convince not convey).

It should be noted that eye contact has zero validity in detecting deception.

I think most of the detection of deception training is focused on the wrong things and too complicated for the layman. Trying to detect deception through micro facial expressions is just too hard to do for most people. Interpreting body language and eye movement produces too many false positives to be reliable.

The most reliable way to detect deception, in my opinion, is to analyze what people say and how they say it.

I come to this conclusion because of my experience as a criminal investigator who conducted thousands of interviews; my time as an interviewer/interrogator in Guantanamo Bay, Cuba and in Iraq; and my years teaching detection of deception at the FBI Academy and internationally.

Deceptive Language Analysis

Based on my research and experience, I developed what I call Deceptive Language Analysis (DLA). DLA is a technique to detect deception by analyzing written and verbal statements of perpetrators, witnesses, and victims. It is a process by which each word and phrase is analyzed and interpreted to gain insight into the writer's or speaker's motivations and actions.

Notice that nowhere are we looking for The Lie. We are looking at the areas of a statement that have elements of deception, the parts of a statement that make one ask why a word or phrase is used, or why there is a lack of detail or too much non-essential information. If we try to find The Lie, we will not see the deceptive words or phrases used. We are too busy trying to find The Lie, that ah-ha moment where we can nail them on their lie. When we do that, we don't see the indicators of deception staring us in the face.

Although I have used DLA most commonly in criminal investigations, DLA is just as applicable in business and our everyday lives.

Wouldn't it be nice to be able to better assess truthfulness and detect verbal deception when we interview the new babysitter?

Or the eighteen-year-old boy coming to pick up your daughter for a first date?

How about when we talk to the contractor building the new deck who is late on the project?

Or the boss regarding the raise you want and deserve that he doesn't seem to want to give you?

How about when counseling your subordinate about their lack of performance?

Consider how important it could be to know when someone is being deceptive in negotiations or during a sales pitch.

DLA can be used in employee-screening interviews, counseling sessions, disciplinary proceedings, resolving employee disputes, and family conflicts.

DLA can assist coaches, counselors, mentors, or anyone who interviews people for a living.

DLA, in my mind, is not only a valuable protection for you, your family, and your business but also a tool to make us all better communicators.

A Brief History of the Detection of Deception

Throughout ancient history, many techniques were used to assess credibility and to better detect deception. Most were cruel, some monstrously so, and almost all were ineffective.

These ancient methods fall into three categories: trial by torture, trial by combat, and trial by ordeal.

Trial by Torture

Trial by torture is probably the best-known method and has been depicted in many movies and television programs. The death scene in *Braveheart*, where Mel Gibson, as William Wallace, is being drawn and quartered is a classic case of trial by torture. The purpose of trial by torture is to make the presumed guilty party confess his or her guilt.

In Rome, trial by torture was used for the confirmation of truthfulness and was a widespread practice that spared few. By using trial by torture as a truth-confirmation tool, it meant that even witnesses were tortured.

The Spanish Inquisition was almost exclusively based on trial by torture. Torture was used to detect hidden crimes against the Catholic Church. Unfortunately, people accused by the church were presumed guilty, which led to the use of very cruel methods of torture to force the confessions.

I think we can all agree that trial by torture is a less-than-optimal means of assessing credibility and detecting deception.

Trial by Combat

Trial by combat was based largely on Divine Judgment. It was the let-God-sort-it-out mentality. The premise of trial by combat was that the accused would do battle to determine who was truthful and who was deceptive. The winner of these contests would be deemed truthful, and the loser deemed guilty. With a system such as this, it is assumed that adversaries would defend themselves, but you would be wrong. If the accused was unable to defend him or herself, such as a woman, she could hire a professional fighter to take her place in combat. Later, it became customary to substitute contestants with professional combatants, and a whole class of professional fighters came about to fill this market need. Some efforts were taken to ensure the professional combatants were at least comparable in age, skill level, size, and strength. Heck of a system!

Trial by Ordeal

This brings us to trial by ordeal. Trial by ordeal, like trial by combat, relied on intervention by God. The basic idea of trial by ordeal is that the accused is forced to endure a physical test and, if they survive the test unscathed, then they have been judged innocent by God.

Some examples of trial by ordeal were:

- Trial by hot iron, where the accused had to carry a red-hot piece of metal at least nine feet without being burned.

- Trial by fire, where the accused must walk on hot coals or stand on a flaming pyre and not be burned in the process.

- Trial by water, where the accused is bound in the fetal position and then thrown into a body of water. If the accused sinks, they are deemed innocent; if they float, they are guilty. The guilty are then retrieved from the water and executed. I wonder how many innocents drowned. Talk about a no-win situation.

- Trial by hot water, where the arm is plunged into a pot of boiling water, often to grasp a stone or ring at the bottom of the pot. If the accused's arm if not scalded by the water, they are considered innocent. Pretty sure this method produced a one hundred percent guilty rate!

These and many more trials where used throughout Europe, Africa, and Asia until the Middle Ages.

As you can see, these early methods of deception detection were unreliable and based on some faulty logic. Thankfully, we have progressed beyond these antiquated methods.

Today, we have the polygraph, sodium pentothal, and voice stress analysis as tools to assist in the detection of deception. Unfortunately, not many people have access to these tools. As I said earlier, DLA is both portable and practical. Anyone can learn it and use it everywhere, with anyone.

But the first thing we have to do to detect deception is to master the hardest part of communication: listening to others.

CHAPTER 2:

Listening with Curiosity

The biggest roadblock to good communications is our collective inattentiveness. We just don't listen. We are distracted with our phones. Our lives are so busy that we can't take time to be in the now. We are always thinking about what is coming up next.

If we would just slow down and listen with curiosity, we would learn so much about what is being said and who is saying it.

I say listen with curiosity, because if you are curious about something you listen closely and actively. If you want to learn how to replace the battery in your key fob, you may watch a YouTube video like I did recently. When watching that video, I listened closely to the steps involved because I was invested in the process and wanted to fix my key fob. I listened with curiosity. If I was listening to a video for entertainment, I know I would have been less attentive because it just wouldn't have been as important to me.

When you are curious and searching for an answer, you are actively listening. You are listening with curiosity.

Passive listening means you hear a speaker say something, but you don't process what is being said. You are not curious.

Daniel Goldman, author of the *New York Times* best seller *Emotional Intelligence* says that "the greatest gift we can give is the gift of paying attention". No one wants to be ignored or have their thoughts and opinions dismissed. By paying attention, people will open up to you.

The reason why I have had success interviewing people is because I make the conscious investment of building rapport. I say investment, because rapport building takes time and effort. It can be hard work. Some people are easier to bond with than others, but common ground can be found with everyone.

Let me tell you a story.

I worked as an FBI interrogator in Iraq in 2007. I interviewed people who were captured on the battlefield for intelligence. Most had extreme animosity toward the American forces and were uncooperative.

Most people think the job of the interrogator is to get confessions. In my opinion, my job as an interrogator is to change the interviewee's mindset from uncooperative to cooperative. Once they are cooperative, the information will be forthcoming. So, my interviews and interrogations are always rapport based.

One of the people I interviewed was a one-legged taxi driver from Baghdad named Abdullah (not his true name). Abdullah used his taxi to transport explosive material used for IEDs. He lost his leg when some of the explosives he transported accidentally denoted.

I was partnered with an FBI agent from Los Angeles named Brian. I would describe Brian as a shorter version of Matthew McConaughey. He was cool and charismatic, with a bit of a surfer-dude vibe. It is impossible to not like Brian. During the course of several interviews, Abdullah fell under Brian's spell.

Brian and I spent a lot of time building rapport with Abdullah. We talked about family, sports, food, cars, and his life. We brought food from the mess hall, and sat on the floor and broke bread with him. We listened with curiosity and waited.

Picture this. You have me—a guy from the mountains of East Tennessee, a west coast surfer dude, and a one-legged Iraqi bomber finding common ground and bonding. It worked because we listened, which led to rapport, which led to cooperation.

Long story short, when it came time for Abdullah to show us where the explosives were being stored, he initially resisted. He claimed ignorance. Brian tried coaxing the needed information out of Abdulla but no dice. Brian feigned disappointment and aggravation with Abdullah's lack of cooperation. Brian loudly closed his notebook and told Abdullah that he was done talking to him.

After watching this little drama play out, I finally told Abdullah he was disrespecting his friendship with Brian. I reminded him how much he cared for Brian and how he was killing their relationship by lying to us. Then I shut up. I could see that Abdullah was upset and near tears.

We sat quietly for a couple of minutes and then Abdullah said, "Turn on your computer. I'll show you where the explosives are stored."

He decided that his friendship with Brian was more important to him than resisting us. Without the rapport building, we would never have gotten this information.

Based on the intelligence provided by Abdullah, military operations were launched, several explosive caches were found and American lives saved.

Because we listened with curiosity and built rapport, we were able to move Abdullah from uncooperative to cooperative.

The primary reasons why we don't listen are:

- We don't care.
- It's hard work.
- Our ego.

We Don't Care

I know it sounds harsh, but the truth is we don't listen because we just don't care. We don't care to get to know people outside of our normal orbit. Heck, we barely know the people in our orbit.

We like to blame technology for keeping us distracted. Granted, studies show that social media, which we access with our smart phones, is addictive. Smart phones are a part of our world and they are never going away. Staying connected is of paramount importance to us. Or at least we think so.

But blaming technology is an easy out. I think we really just don't care. We aren't interested in what anyone other than ourselves has to say on any subject. With the advance of technology, we have become progressively more self-involved and isolated. We have become disconnected due to a lot of reasons, but the biggest is that we just aren't interested in each other.

To listen with curiosity and become a good communicator requires us to actually be interested in what the other person has to say.

Have you ever introduced yourself to someone and then they call you by a different name? And no matter how many times you correct them, they still call you by the wrong name. Well, I have.

When I lived in East Amherst, New York, a nice couple moved in next door. Chuck was a retired cop and worked for the University of Buffalo Police Department. I introduced myself telling him my name was Frank. Chuck then proceeded to call me Brian. I corrected Chuck saying, "No, no, my name is Frank." Chuck acknowledged this.

The next time I saw Chuck was approximately a week later. At this chance meeting, Chuck called me Brian. Once again, I told him my name was Frank.

The next time I saw Chuck, he was in his yard. I waved at him and he said, "Hi, Brian." It was at this time that I decided I was a character named Brian in the movie Chuck called his life. So, I responded, "Hey, Chuck."

For the next two years, I was Brian to Chuck, until one fateful day. It turned out that Chuck had just been offered the job to be the head of security at Florida Agricultural and Mechanical University (FAMU). In preparation for his upcoming move, Chuck needed to trim some tree branches in his back yard but he did not have a ladder tall enough. Of course, I did.

So on that fateful Saturday, Chuck rang my doorbell. I was upstairs when I heard the bell and my wife was in the kitchen. She answered the door, and I heard Chuck say, "Hi, is Brian home?"

I immediately jumped up and by the time I reached the top of the stairs, I heard my wife say, "There is no Brian here."

Chuck then inquired, "Your husband, Brian?" and pointed at me at the top of the stairs. Before I could avert this embarrassing moment for all involved, my wife then let the cat out of the bag, and stated, "My husband's name is Frank." Oh, boy!

I immediately intervened and stepped out to see what Chuck wanted. The look on his face said, *Is your wife crazy?* and *Doesn't your wife know your name and why not?* Chuck then asked, "Is your name Frank?" I told him yes, and then he asked the big question, "Why did you let me call you Brian for all this time?" I explained to Chuck that I corrected him twice when he called me Brian, yet he never listened and continued to call me Brian. So, I just decided that I was Brian in his world.

It was awkward and somewhat embarrassing, granted. But when people don't care enough to listen, I set my correction rule to two times and after that, they can call me whatever they want.

It's Hard Work

Listening with curiosity can be hard work, especially when the speaker is off-putting. There is something about their voice, body language, or physical appearance that is distracting or unpleasant. We would like to think we are all above these petty feeling, but we really aren't. The best we can hope for is enough self-awareness to know when we are distracted by these things and be intentional in our listening.

Daniel Kahneman, author of *Thinking, Fast and Slow*, says that listening creates a large cognitive load which tires the brain and leads to inattentiveness and distraction. According to Kahneman, doing two things at the same time is difficult and he uses the example of calculating a math problem while listening. He says if you try to calculate seventeen times twenty-four while listening, you will stop listening to the speaker while doing the calculation. The cognitive load is too great to do both at the same time.

Our Ego

Beyond not caring, the other big reason we don't listen is our ego gets in the way.

The best interviewers, whether they are criminal investigators, HR professionals, counselors, or coaches, are the ones who leave their egos at the door.

Our egos are the genesis of our internal bias. I could go into a long dissertation on biases, of which there are many, that contribute to our poor listening skills. I could talk about confirmation bias or the halo effect, but I think it is more productive to address these ego-driven biases in terms we can all relate to.

We have all met these people and occasionally, been that person.

- The One Upper

  The One Upper is the person who always has a story to top your story. When you are talking, you can feel that they can hardly wait for you to finish your story so they can tell their story, which is always a little bigger and better. They quickly pick up the thread of the story you're telling, stop listening, and then immediately go to their mental catalog of stories on this subject and pull one out to use to one up you.

- I'm better than you

Have you ever met someone who knows they are better than you? They are more important than you because of their position in society or their career. When you are talking to them, they are always scanning the room for someone else to talk to who is more important than you. Someone more of their ilk. These guys aren't listening to you because you don't deserve their attention. You're nice enough, but really who are you and how important is anything you have to say?

- Smartest guy in the room

I have seen this play out numerous times during my law-enforcement career. The agent interviewing a perp is so focused on showing how much they know and how smart they are that they barely listen to the perp's answers to their questions. They are more focused on their next question than the answer to the question that has just been asked. They want to show they are in control and that they are the intellectually superior. They are ego driven. They are listening to their ego more than they are listening to the person they are interviewing. To be a successful interviewer and to really listen, the ego must be set aside.

- I already know the story

Sometimes we think we already know what someone is going to tell us. Our prior experience with this person or a similar situation leads us to believe we already know the story. We are just looking for confirmation. We only listen for the information that supports our opinions, and we discard the rest. This is also called confirmation bias.

- I don't like you

Have you ever tried to listen to someone you don't like? It's really hard to do. I know that I have a hard time doing it. It's so easy to dismiss what is being said because of who the messenger is. As the listener, you have already written the story that they don't know what they are talking about and their information is not to be taken seriously. Once again, your ego has taken over and you are listening to it more than the speaker.

- I really like you

   This is the flip side of I don't like you. Critical listening goes out the window because of your favorable opinion of the speaker. You only listen for the good parts and dismiss the rest. This is called the Halo Effect.

- The problem solver

   This is a combination of the smartest guy in the room and I already know the story. When you are placed in the position of being a problem solver, your ego takes over. You are going to be the hero and solve the problem. You already know what needs to be done and you can't wait to provide the answer to their problem.

I've been married long enough to know that when my wife has had a hard day at work, she wants to just tell me about her day and her interactions with people on the job. She isn't looking for a solution. She just wants to be heard. If I am being the problem solver, I am not really listening, I'm just waiting my turn to talk and solve her problem. Wrong move!

Being Intentional

Listening with curiosity requires you to be intentional. You, as the listener, have to make a decision to listen or not. When I tell myself to listen with curiosity before I do an interview, it reminds me to get in the right frame of mind. People will tell you everything you need to know if you really listen with curiosity.

Communication is a two-way street: sending and receiving. If you only send and don't receive, you are a prime target for anyone who wants to deceive and take you for a ride.

In his book, *Never Split the Difference. Negotiating as if your life depends on it,* Chris Voss, former FBI Hostage Negotiator, believes the person doing the listening during a conversation has the most control, not the person doing the talking. Voss reasons that "the talker is revealing information while the listener, if he is trained well, is directing the conversation towards his own goals. He's harnessing the talker's energy for his own goals." I couldn't agree more.

The most reliable way to build rapport, get to know someone and know when you are being BS'ed, is to listen with curiosity. Listening with curiosity will make you a better communicator.

CHAPTER 3:

Balanced versus Unbalanced Statements

Tuesday, October 25, 1994

Susan has a problem. She is married to a good man that she doesn't love and in love with a man she isn't married to.

She's a small-town girl who wants much more than what the manager of the local Winn-Dixie supermarket can give her. Tom, on the other hand, can help her live out her dreams. He is the son and heir to one of the wealthiest families in Union County, South Carolina. Susan has relentlessly pursued Tom, letting him know of her interest in him. Tom, knowing Susan's reputation for being promiscuous, has had a couple of dates with Susan, which have ended with them having sex. For Tom, it's business as usual. For Susan, it's love (or close enough). But now Tom is starting to get cold feet.

Susan looks at her two sons, Michael and Alex, and knows that they are what is blocking her path to happiness with Tom. She knows this because Tom has told her that he has no interest in having children. And to make things worse, Tom is seeing Susan Brown, and Susan is deathly afraid that her dreams are quickly evaporating.

Susan has decided. She gathers up the boys and tells them they are going for a drive.

A drive that will end at the John D. Long Lake boat ramp.

There's a saying, "If you begin well, you end well." With that in mind, let's talk about the first step in detecting deception.

All statements, whether verbal or written, consist of three parts: The Prologue, the Incident, and the Epilogue, also known as the PIE.

The Prologue (P) is the beginning of the statement. It is where the writer/speaker sets the table on what happened. It is the beginning of the story.

The Incident (I) is the meat and potatoes of the statement. It is the part of the statement that answers the question "What happened and who was involved?"

The Epilogue (E) is the last part of a statement, and it tells us about the aftermath of the Incident. It is how the story ends.

The first thing I do to determine the truthfulness of a statement is compare the relative lengths of each part of the statement. This is known as calculating the PIE. Once the PIE is calculated, you can easily determine if a statement is balanced or unbalanced.

When analyzing a statement, always identify the main topic of the statement. What is the statement about? If I ask a victim of a sexual assault to write a statement about what happened, I always write on the top of the first page what question I want answered. In this case, I would write, "Tell me about the sexual assault." This way the victim knows what they are supposed to write about. I don't tell them how much detail to include in their statement. I want them to make that decision, but I want there to be no doubt what the statement is to be about. How much detail they give and where they provide it is up to them.

If they give a lot of detail in the prologue and little in the incident, that is a strong sign of deception. Why? Because you have told them what the statement is about, yet they choose to give little detail about the most important part of the statement. That is suspicious and should make you ask yourself *Why? Why isn't the writer giving the most information about the most important part of the statement? Why aren't they giving the most information to the investigators to find the culprit? Why are they providing more detail leading up to Incident and after the Incident itself? Is the topic they are writing about different from the Incident? What is the writer most concerned with?*

Different schools of thought have emerged concerning the balance as an indicator of veracity.

Don Rabon, author of *Investigative Discourse Analysis*, believes a statement is balanced when each of the parts of the PIE make up approximately 33% of a statement.

Avinoam Sapir, creator of Scientific Content Analysis (S.C.A.N.), purports that a statement is balanced when the PIE is roughly twenty-five percent prologue, fifty percent incident, and twenty-five percent epilogue.

Wendell "Buddy" Rudacille, author of *Identifying Lies in Disguise* thinks a balanced statement consists of twenty percent prologue, sixty percent incident, and twenty percent epilogue.

I don't place a specific percentage for each part of the PIE, but in my opinion, statements where the incident makes up most of the statement are the best indicator of a truthful statement. At a minimum, each part of the statement should be relatively equal.

The more details someone gives when telling a story, the more likely they are telling the truth. As I have stated before, it is hard to keep a long, complex lie straight. Remembering details that you will have to repeat over and over consistently is very challenging, and the normal person will try to avoid fabricating the story out of whole cloth.

Let's take a look at a statement to give you an example of how to calculate the PIE.

1. When the wake-up call came at 6 AM, I was already up because I

2. don't sleep well in motels. I had been watching early news; they

3. were talking about the terrible airline crash; they are still finding

4. body parts. I then took a shower (it was a quick one because the

5. water was not very hot), got dressed and went to the lobby for

6. their continental breakfast. I had a doughnut (greasy but good) and

7. a cup of coffee. I then went back to my room, checked to make sure

8. I had packed everything, got my bags, and put them in the trunk of

9. the car. I then went back to the lobby to check out. I got another

10. cup of coffee while I was there. I then used my Visa card to pay for the

11. room, but the system was down and it took some time to

12. verify it. I then walked to my car and as I was putting my key in

13. the lock a man poked something in my back and told me not to

14. move. He took my keys and my wallet and told me to get in the car

15. and lie face down and not move. I did as I was told until I was sure

16. he was gone. I then went back to the lobby and had them call 911

17. and waited for you to get here.

This statement is seventeen lines long. When calculating the PIE, the first thing we look for is the incident section of the statement. The rule of thumb is the incident section starts where the person in the statement realizes that there is danger or something amiss. The incident section ends when that person realizes that the danger has passed.

In this statement, the incident section starts on line thirteen at "a man poked something in my back." The incident section ends on line sixteen where the writer says he was sure the assailant had left.

So, if we place the incident box in the statement, it would look something like this:

1. When the wake-up call came at 6 AM, I was already up because I
2. don't sleep well in motels. I had been watching early news; they
3. were talking about the terrible airline crash; they are still finding
4. body parts. I then took a shower (it was a quick one because the
5. water was not very hot), got dressed and went to the lobby for
6. their continental breakfast. I had a doughnut (greasy but good) and
7. a cup of coffee. I then went back to my room, checked to make sure
8. I had packed everything, got my bags, and put them in the trunk of
9. the car. I then went back to the lobby to check out. I got another
10. cup of coffee while I was there. I then used my Visa card to pay
11. for the room, but the system was down and it took some time
12. to verify it. I then walked to my car and as I was putting my key in
13. the lock *a man poked something in my back and told me not to*
14. *move. He took my keys and my wallet and told me to get in the car*
15. *and lie face down and not move. I did as I was told until I was sure*
16. *he was gone.* I then went back to the lobby and had them call 911
17. and waited for you to get here.

To calculate the PIE, divide the number of lines that compose the prologue, incident, and the epilogue by the number of lines of the entire statement. In this case it would be:

$$12 \div 17 = 0.70 \text{ P} = 70\%$$

$$3 \div 17 = 0.18 \text{ I} = 18\%$$

$$2 \div 17 = 0.12 \text{E} = 12\%$$

Is the statement balanced? Obviously not. The prologue is far too long. Consider this: if you were robbed by an armed assailant, would that not be the most significant thing that happened to you that day, maybe your entire year? Probably.

If the cops asked you to provide a statement about how you were robbed, where would you start the story? When you got up at six in the morning or when you walked out to your car? I submit that most reasonable people would start the story at the point when they walked out to their car. Everything leading up to the robbery is extraneous information.

Don't be fooled by the term *extraneous information*. Extraneous sounds like it is unimportant, but extraneous information, as you will learn later, often contains valuable information about the writer/speaker and their mindset.

Susan Smith Statement

The opening vignette in this chapter was about Susan Smith, the South Carolina mother who drowned her two sons in the John D. Long Lake by leaving them strapped in their car seats while she let her car slowly submerge into the lake.

Susan was a small-town girl from Union, South Carolina, married to David Smith, the manager of the local Winn-Dixie. Susan worked at CONSCO, a manufacturing company where she met Tom Findlay, son of the owner of CONSCO and considered the most eligible bachelor in Union County.

Findlay and Susan came from two different worlds. Findlay was from a world of privilege and Susan was from a world of dysfunction.

Smith's parents divorced when she was young and her father committed suicide when she was fourteen. Smith's mother remarried and Smith's new stepfather eventually sexually assaulted her when she was a teenager.

To escape her unfortunate home life, Smith married David Smith at a young age and quickly had two children, Michael and Alex.

But Smith was promiscuous. She had a short-lived sexual affair with Findlay, which he considered nothing more than a fling. Smith saw her relationship with Findlay as a way out of a bleak and meager existence, if she could only land him.

Shortly before killing her children, Smith sent a letter to Findlay stating she hoped to continue their relationship. Findlay replies to her letter telling her that he has no interest in continuing his sexual relationship with her, citing the fact that she has children and his lack of interest in having children in his life.

Here are those letters.

SUSAN SMITH'S LETTER TO TOM FINDLAY

Dear Tom,

Just a note to say thank you for everything. I could never express in words how much you mean to me. I will always treasure our friendship and all of the many wonderful memories we have made.

I want you to know that I have never felt with anyone, the way I feel when I'm with you. I have never felt so needed. You are a very special person and that is part of why making love to you is so wonderful.

I know how you feel about our relationship and I respect that. I'm appreciative of your honesty with me. I do want us to be friends forever and I'll never let anything happen that would change that.

I do hope that we will be able to date some and be together again someday, but if we never made love again, my feelings for you would not change because having you as my friend is worth more than sex could ever be worth.

Once again, I'm sorry for Sat. night and would take it back in a (heart-shaped design) beat if I could. I really wanted to be with you and hated that I wasn't.

Thank you for being there for me through all the rough times. You are a true friend. I want you to know that I will always love and care for you for the rest of my life. **You** are the best friend anyone could ever have.

Well, I hope I said everything right. The bottom line is: I'm glad we are friends and if that is all we can be, then we will just have to do a hell of a job of being that. Who knows what the future holds for our relationship. I'm just going to live one day at a time.

One more thing before I go, please don't ever hesitate to call me if you ever need **anything**! I will always be here for you!

Friends Forever, (a heart-shaped design on each side of the words)

Susan

Tom Findlay's Response

Dear Susan,

I hope you don't mind, but I think clearer when I am typing, so this letter is being written on my computer.

This is a difficult letter for me to write because I know how much you think of me. And I want you to know that I am flattered that you have such a high opinion of me. Susan, I value our friendship very much. You are one of the few people on this earth that I feel I can tell anything. You are intelligent, beautiful, sensitive, understanding, and possess many other wonderful qualities that I and many other men appreciate. You will, without a doubt, make some lucky man a great wife. But unfortunately, it won't be me.

Even though you think we have much in common, we are vastly different. We have been raised in two totally different environments, and therefore, think totally different. That's not to say that I was raised better than you or vice versa, it just means that we come from two different backgrounds.

When I started dating Laura, I knew our backgrounds were going to be a problem. Right before I graduated from Auburn University in 1990, I broke up with a girl (Alison) that I had been dating for over two years. I loved Alison very much and we were very compatible. Unfortunately, we wanted different things out of life. She wanted to get married and have children before the age of 28, and I did not. This conflict spurred our breakup, but we have remained friends through the years. After Alison, I was very hurt. I decided not to fall for anyone again until I was ready to make a long commitment.

For my first two years in Union, I dated very little. In fact, I can count the number of dates I had on one hand. But then Laura came along. We met at CONSCO, and I fell for her like "a ton of bricks." Things were great at first and remained good for a long time, but I knew deep in my heart that she was not the one for me. People tell me that when you find the person that you will want to spend the rest of your life with ... you will know it. Well, even though I fell enlove *(sic)* with Laura, I had my doubts about a long and lasting commitment, but I never said anything, and I eventually hurt her very, very deeply. I won't do that again.

Susan, I could really fall for you. You have so many endearing qualities about you, and I think that you are a terrific person. But like I have told you before, there are some things about you that aren't suited for me, and yes, I am speaking about your children. I'm sure that your kids are good kids, but it really wouldn't matter how good they may be ... the fact is, I just don't want children. These feelings may change one day, but I doubt it. With all of the crazy, mixed-up things that take place in this world today, I just don't have the desire to bring another life into it. And I don't want to be responsible for anyone elses children, either. But I am very thankful that there are people like you who are not so selfish as I am, and don't mind bearing the responsibility of children. If everyone thought the way that I do, our species would eventually become extinct.

But our differences go far beyond the children issue. We are just two totally different people, and eventually, those differences would cause us to break-up. Because I know myself so well, I am sure of this.

But don't be discouraged. There is someone out there for you. In fact, it's probably someone that you may not know at this time or that you may know but would never expect. Either way, before you settle down with anyone again, there is something you need to do. Susan, because you got pregnant and married at such an early age, you missed out on much of your youth. I mean, one minute you were a kid, and the next minute you were having kids. Because I come from a place where everyone had the desire and the money to go to college, having the responsibility of children at such a young age is beyond my comprehension. Anyhow, my advice to you is to wait and be very choosy about your next relationship. I can see this may be a bit difficult for you because you are a bit boy crazy, but as the proverb states "good things come to those who wait." I am not saying you shouldn't go out and have a good time. In fact, I think you should do just that … have a good time and capture some of that youth that you missed out on. But just don't get seriously involved with anyone until you have done the things in life that you want to do, first. Then the rest will fall in place.

Susan, I am not mad at you about what happened this weekend. Actually, I am very thankful. As I told you, I was starting to let my heart warm up to the idea of us going out as more than just friends. But seeing you kiss another man put things back into perspective. I remembered how I hurt Laura, and I won't let that happen again; and therefore, I can't let myself get close to you. We will always be friends, but our relationship will never go beyond that of friendship. And as for your relationship with B. Brown, of course you have to make your own decisions in life, but remember … you have to live with the consequences also. Everyone is held accountable for their actions, and I would hate for people to perceive you as an unreputable person. If you want to catch a nice guy like me one day, you have to act like a nice girl. And you know, nice girls don't sleep with married men. Besides, I want you to feel good about yourself, and I am afraid that if you sleep with B. Brown or any other married man for that matter, you will lose your self-respect. I know I did when we were messing around earlier this year. So please, think about your actions before you do anything you will regret. I care for you, but also care for Susan Brown and I would hate to see anyone get hurt. Susan may say that she wouldn't care (copy unintelligible) husband had an affair, but you and I know, that is not true.

Anyhow, as I have already told you, you are a very special person. And don't let anyone tell you or make you feel any different. I see so much potential in you, but only you can make it happen. Don't settle for mediocre in life, go for it all and only settle for the best … I do. I haven't told you this, but I am extremely proud of you for going to school. I am a firm believer in higher education, and once you obtain a degree from college, there is not stopping you. And don't let these idiot boys from Union make you feel like you are not capable or slow you down. After you graduate, you will be able to go anywhere you want in this world. And if you ever wanted to get a good job in Charlotte, my father is the right person to know. He and Koni know everyone who is anyone in the business world in Charlotte. And if I can ever help you with anything, don't hesitate to ask.

Well, this letter must come to an end. It is 11:50 p.m. and I am getting very sleepy. But I wanted to write you this letter because you are the one who is always making the effort for me, and I wanted to return the friendship. I've appreciated it when you have dropped me nice little notes, or cards, or the present at Christmas, and it is about time that I start putting a little effort into our friendship. Which reminds me, I thought long and hard about getting you something for your birthday, but I decided not to because I wasn't sure what you might think. Now I am sorry I didn't get you anything, so you can expect something from me at Christmas. But **do not** buy me anything for Christmas. All I want from you is a nice, sweet card ... I'll cherish that more than any store (copy illegible) present.

Again, you will **always** have my friendship. And your friendship is one that I will always look upon with sincere affection.

Tom

p.s. It's late, so please don't count off for spelling or grammar.

I believe Findlay's letter is what set Smith on the path to murder her children.

On October 25, 1994, Smith loaded her two sons, Michael and Alex, in her red Mazda, strapped them into their child seats, and drove to the John D.

Long Lake. She knew where the boat ramp was, and drove partially down it and parked. She then got out of her car and let it roll down the ramp into the lake. As she stood there watching, she could hear the terrified cries of her two sons. She then went to the nearest house and called the police.

The following is Smith's first statement given to law enforcement after the incident.

1 I arrived home around 6:00 p.m. on
2 Tuesday, October 25, 1994. It had been
3 an upsetting day for me. When I
4 walked in the door, my phone was ringing,
5 but before I could answer it, they
6 hung up. I have call return on my
7 phone so I dialed back and it was
8 my mom. I asked her if she was
9 going to be home because I might
10 come over. (When I am upset, I have
11 to go somewhere or do something). She
12 told me what she was going to Nick's
13 ball game at 7:00 and it would
14 probably only last an hour so she
15 would be back home some time after
16 8:00. She asked me if she wanted me
17 to just let her come by my house
18 and I told her no what I would
19 rather come see her. (She didn't know
20 what I was upset) We ended the
21 conversation with me planning on coming
22 to her house. I hung up the phone
23 and went into the living room w/ Michael
24 & Alex. If I recall correctly, he put a
25 movie in the VCR. I went into the
26 kitchen and tried to find them

27   Something to eat. I decided to fix
28   them ~~order~~ a pizza. They played in
29   the meantime and I played with
30   them. Because of my conversation with
31   Tom earlier, I was concerned about
32   him and I knew that he was at
33   Hickory Nuts with Susan Brown. So I
34   called Hickory Nuts to talk to Susan
35   to see how Tom was. ~~One~~ I could
36   tell by talking to her that she couldn't
37   say much about Tom because Tom was
38   sitting beside her. She told me she
39   would call me later and talk to me.
40   I said O.K. I really don't remember
41   what else I did after that. Before I
42   left that night I also received a call
43   from David. He said he was just
44   calling to see what we were doing and
45   to just chit chat. He could tell that
46   something was bothering me and he
47   asked me what was wrong. I told
48   him that I couldn't tell him. He
49   said you can tell me anything and I
50   said not this. We ended the conversation
51   with him saying that if I needed him
52   to call him. After that phone call, I

53 began to prepare ~~them~~ a diaper bag
54 for Michael & Alex. Since I was
55 going to my mom's I was just going
56 to go ahead and give them a bath
57 at her house so I got them some
58 pajamas ready and I fixed Alex a
59 bottle. It was around 8:00 or a little
60 after when I left the house. When I
61 left you could tell that I had been
62 crying, so I said we will just ride
63 around a little while ~~????~~ because I
64 didn't want my mom know that I
65 had been upset so we rode around
66 all over Union and up to Jonesville
67 and I was riding I just thought
68 that Michael & Alex hadn't seen
69 Mitch in a while so I asked Michael
70 if he wanted to go see Mitch and he
71 told me yes. So I said to myself
72 we will go see Mitch and I'll call
73 my mom from there and let her know
74 that I wasn't coming over there.
75 Unfortunately I never made it to
76 Mitch's. I had stopped at the red
77 light at Monarch Mill and while I
78 was waiting for the light to change

79 a black man jumped in my car, put
80 a gun to my side and said "Drive or
81 I'll kill you." I went into hysterics
82 and started screaming why are you
83 doing this? what do you want? He just
84 told me to shut up and drive or
85 he would kill me. michael asked me
86 who that man was and what was
87 wrong. I tried to comfort him and
88 tell him that everything would be
89 O.K. The black man allowed me to
90 talk to michael and Alex a couple
91 of times but when he told me that
92 was enough. I continued to drive and
93 was praying to the Lord to take
94 care of me and my children. Out of
95 nowhere, the black man told me to
96 stop. It was odd to me that he
97 was asking me to stop right
98 there in the middle of the road on
99 that highway. I questioned him about
100 stopping and he told me right quick
101 again to stop the car right now! I
102 was going to
103 pull over on the side of the road and
104 stop but he told me no, to stop right

105 here. He then told me to get out
106 of the car *or I'm going to kill you* and I opened my car
107 door and told him what I have to
108 get my babies and as he was moving
109 over to the driver's seat he was
110 pushing me out of the car and he
111 told me that he didn't have time and
112 I screamed and begged for him to
113 please let me get my children and
114 he said again that he didn't have
115 time but told me that he would
116 not hurt my children. He shut the
117 door and took off. I dropped to the
118 road like a ton of bricks, screaming
119 for someone to please help me! I
120 went totally numb. I then jumped up
121 and started running up the road
122 continuing to scream for help. I ran to
123 the closest house that had lights on.
124 I could barely see because it was so
125 dark. I got on this front porch and
126 I banged on the door continuing to cry
127 for help. A lady and man opened the
128 door and saw that I was in trouble
129 but I could hardly tell her what was
130 wrong. She took me into her house

131 and tryed to calm me enough so I could
132 tell her what had happened. Once
133 they knew what had happened, they
134 immediately phoned the police. As I
135 sat in that lady's house, I prayed and
136 prayed that my Children be o.k. I
137 was devastated, I was hysterical, I
138 couldn't understand why!!

Smith's handwritten statement is 138 lines long. Using what we know about calculating the PIE, where does the incident begin? Where is the first mention of the carjacking?

The alleged carjacking begins on line seventy-nine when the "black man" jumped into her car while waiting at a traffic light. The incident ends on line 117 when Smith stated, "He shut the door and took off."

So, the prologue is seventy-eight lines long.

The incident is thirty-six lines long.

The epilogue is twenty-two lines long.

$$78 \div 138 = 0.565 \; P = 57\%$$

$$36 \div 138 = 0.260 \; I = 26\%$$

$$22 \div 138 = 0.159 \; E = 16\%$$

The statement is wildly out of balance.

Smith spends the first seventy-eight lines providing extraneous information. When I read this statement during my classes, I always stop at the end of each page and remind my audience that she is supposed to be telling the cops about the carjacking and kidnapping of her two sons. Any normal, truthful person when asked to provide a statement about the kidnapping of your children would start with something like, "I was sitting at the traffic light in Union when…." Not Smith. She gave tons of irrelevant information without answering the main question, "Tell me about the carjacking." Although I am not sure what the investigators asked her to write the statement about, she knew what it was about.

She used extraneous information to justify why she was out driving with her sons near the lake, to appear cooperative and to buy time. She knew she had to fabricate a lie about a black man carjacking her and kidnapping her sons. She wanted to delay telling that stressful lie, and used extraneous information as the means to do it.

Lying is hard. There are many more aspects of this statement that indicate deception. These will be addressed in subsequent chapters.

Quick Tips:

1.   All statement can be divided into three parts:

Prologue—before the incident

Incident—the event or incident

Epilogue—after the event or incident

2.   A statement is balanced if the three parts are generally equal in size or when the incident is the largest portion of the statement.

3.   If the prologue is longer than the incident, this is a possible sign of deception.

4.   Identify the main topic of discussion.

Ask:

- What seems to be the person's main concern?
- What does he/she talk about?
- Do they talk about something other than the main topic?

5.   Extraneous information is used usually to justify the writer's actions, to appear cooperative and to buy time.

CHAPTER 4:

Indicators of Veracity

Testimony from an elderly woman named Miss Hattie in Edwards, Mississippi, who was an attempted rape victim.

There appeared this man standing in my bedroom door with a cap turned backwards on his head and both fists balled up and shoulders slumped over like that. And I laid there and I squinched my eyes, to make sure I was awake, and he was standing there trying to focus on me. And I sat straight up in bed and I said oh my God, my God, and he ran over to the bed as fast as he could and shoved me with his hand open in my chest and he shoved me back in bed. And he said ok, I'm gonna' take my clothes off, he said, you listen, I'm gonna' take my clothes off, he said, and if you breathe loud, bitch, you're dead. I said ok, and I started back to saying Lord, have mercy, every time I'd say something he said shut up bitch. I said ok, ok. He pulled his shoes off, he didn't bend, he slipped his shoes off like that, and I'm focusing on his fist to see if he's holding something in his hand. He took his shirt off and threw it on the floor. He told me step by step what he was taking off. I'm taking off my pants, he slipped out of his pants, and he crawled up into bed. He crawled up to the top of the bed and he sat in a sitting position. I have a tall headboard on my bed, and he sat in a sitting position. And I slid down in bed and put one foot, braced one of my feet on the floor, my right foot, and I said where is it, where is it, and I got it, I grabbed it by my right hand. When I grabbed it, I gave it a yank, and when I yanked, it got twisted all at the same time. And he hit me with his right hand, a hard blow beside the head. And when he hit me, I grabbed a hold to his scrotum with my left hand, and I was twisting it the opposite way. He started to yell, and we fell to the floor. And he hit me a couple of more licks, but they were light licks, he was weakening some then. Then he leaned over across me and bit me on my right shoulder. While he was biting me, I was still hanging on to him and then I got his neck with my mouth and start biting it. Then I thought, well he might have AIDS and I let go of his neck, still holding on to him. And he was tussling and trying to hit me and trying to get out of the way, and I don't know how we managed to get out of the bedroom into the hallway. He was trying to get out and I'm hanging onto him and he was throwing me from one side of the hall wall to the other. I was determined I was not going to turn him loose. So we were going down the hallway, falling from one side to the other, and we got into the living room and, and we both fell, he brought me down right in front of the couch and he leaned back against the couch like this pleading with me, he says, you got me, you got me, please, you got me. I said I know goddamn well I've got you. He said, please, please, you're killing me, you're killing me. I said well, die, son of a bitch, I said die then. I said, son of a bitch, you just won't die for me, will you? And I couldn't get him to die. And he said I can't do nothing; I can't do nothing. Call the police, call the police. I said, do you think I'm stupid enough to turn you lose and call the police? He said well, what am I gonna' do? I said, you gonna' get the goddamn hell out of my house. He said well how can I get out of your house if you won't let me go? He said, how can I get out? I can't get out. I said break out son of a bitch, you broke in, didn't you? And I was still holding him. He said, I can't do nothing. He said, oh, you got me suffering. Lady, you got me suffering. He said, woman, you got me suffering. I said hell, have you thought about how you was gonna' have me suffering? He said, well I can't do nothing. I said, well, that's fine, I said, we'll stay right here until my brother comes. He'll be here at 5:00 anyway. So, I said I've got two locks on my door, a dead bolt lock and a night lock. And I said, damn if you're not going to undo both of them. So, we go to the door, we fumble to the door. He gets up to the lock and he's in so much pain he'd come back down to the floor and I make him get back up to the locks. So he managed to get one loose and

he pulled it and he said I'm out. I said, no, there's another one. He undid that one.
He still thought he was out. I said, the screen door is locked. And he undid the screen
door, he said, I'm out, I'm out. I said no, damnit, come on. You're going to the end
of the porch. I said, I'm taking your ass to the end of the porch. I said, and when I
turn you lose, I'm gonna' go get my gun and I'm gonna' blow your mother fucking
brains out. And I said you nasty, stinking, low down, dirty piece of shit you, and
when I did that, I gave it a twist and I turned him loose. And he made a couple of
steps and then he fell off the steps and he jumped up and he took his right hand and
grabbed down here in his private area, and made a couple of jumps, across the back
of my aunt's car. And I ran into my aunt's room, got her pistol from underneath the
nightstand, ran back to the screen door, and I fired two shots down the hill the way
I saw him go. And then I ran back into the house and dialed 911.

The jury deliberated seven minutes before finding the defendant guilty. He was sentenced to twenty-five years in a Mississippi state prison.

When using DLA, I always evaluate every statement for the presence of three things: unique sensory details, spatial details, and emotions. This chapter will explain unique sensory details and spatial details. Chapter 5 will deal with emotions in statements.

One of the best indicators of deception is the lack of pertinent details when recounting an incident. Statements containing few details, especially unique sensory details, are always suspect. But as stated earlier, it is much easier to remember one's deceptive answer when you don't have to remember those pesky details.

Many studies conducted over the years show that truthful statements contain far more details than fabricated statements and that these details contain more sensory information. (M.K. Johnson, M.A. Foley, A.G. Suengas, & C.L. Raye; *"Phenomenal characteristics of memories for perceived & imagined autobiographical events."* Journal of Experimental Psychology: General, Vol 117 (4), Dec 1988, 371-376)

Why We Remember Things

Emotionally charged events, whether a violent assault, car accident, or incident that had the potential for extreme bodily harm or death, are imprinted in our memories more than average, mundane daily events.

If you ask someone who came of age during the fifties and sixties where they were when they heard about the Kennedy assassination, they can tell you with detail. Ask me and millions of others about the September 11, 2001, attacks and we can tell you with vivid details of where we were when the attacks occurred, who we were with, and many of the things said at the time. These details are etched in our memory banks.

According to molecular scientist John Medina, "Emotionally charged events persist longer in our memories and are recalled with greater accuracy than neutral memories." The amygdala, which is in the frontal cortex of the brain, is loaded with the neurotransmitter dopamine. When a person experiences an emotionally charged event, dopamine is released, which results in improved memory and information processing (John Medina, *Brain Rules*, Pear Press, 2008).

Sensory Memories

The first Indicator of veracity, unique sensory details, are derived from sensory memory. Sensory memory allows an individual to recall in great detail a complex stimulus (an incident) immediately following its presentation (its occurrence). It is a snapshot of the person's sensory impressions regarding a vivid event. Sensory memory has a short retention timeframe, but it is retained long enough to be transferred to short-term (working) memory, and from there to long-term memory.

All five senses (sight, smell, taste, sound, and touch) leave sensory memory imprints on the brain. But three types of sensory memory—iconic, echoic, and haptic—have been researched the most and provide us an insight of how sensory memories work.

Iconic memories are where visual stimuli are stored. When we see something, it is stored as an icon, thus the term iconic memory.

Auditory stimuli, what we hear, is stored in the echoic memory. Echoic memory has a large storage capacity, but for only three to four seconds before being transferred to the working memory.

Haptic memory is the part of the sensory memory regarding the sense of touch. Sensory receptors located throughout the body detect sensations such as pain, pressure, and the feeling of being touched, and are retained for a short period of time before being sent to the working memory.

Short-Term (Working) Memories

In 1974, Alan Baddeley and Graham Hitch proposed a theory exploring how short-term memory transfers information into the working memory. According to Baddeley and Hitch, working memory has three components: a phonological loop, a visuospatial sketchpad, and a central executive function to divide attention between them. In 2000, Baddeley added a fourth component, the episodic buffer, which links information from the phonological loop and the visuospatial sketchpad with time sequencing or chronological ordering to recall memories not just as snapshots but in a sequence like a movie.

The phonological loop is responsible for processing all audio stimuli, what we hear and say. It is a system that deals with language and has two parts: the phonological store, which stores audio memory traces, and the articulatory loop, which can recall those memory traces.

The visuospatial sketchpad is where all visual and spatial information, what we see, is stored. The location of objects and places are retained on the visuospatial sketchpad.

The phonological loop and the visuospatial sketchpad work semi-independently of each other and allow a person to retain more sensory memories when both are engaged simultaneously.

The central executive connects these two systems, linking the working memory to the long-term memory and manages the retrieval of memories.

Transferring memories from the working memory bucket to the long-term memory bucket involves the encoding and consolidation of information, which takes time. Luckily, the longer a memory is in short-term (working) memory, the more likely it will be transferred to long-term memory. Additionally, as noted earlier, the more vivid or emotionally charged a memory is, the greater the retention rate.

Long-Term Memories

Long-term memory is the final, semi-permanent stage of memory. Long-term memories can be subcategorized as explicit and implicit memories.

Explicit memory contains facts, concepts, and events that requires conscious recall of the memories. These memories are explicitly stored in long-term memory, hence the name explicit memory.

Implicit memories are memories for completing actions and procedures. You are using implicit memory when you drive your car to work and do not remember any part of the drive itself. You do not have to consciously recall how to drive your car to get to work.

Explicit memories can be broken down into two parts: semantic memories and episodic memories.

Semantic memories involve abstract factual knowledge like knowing your state's capital or where your child's school is located. It is the type of memories needed to take tests or be good at trivia.

Episodic memories are more contextualized memories. It is where one recalls specific moments or episodes in one's life. As such, these memories also involve emotions and sensations (the five senses) in additional to who, what, when, where, and how. This is where the unique sensory details and spatial details reside.

Unique Sensory Details

So, what is a unique sensory detail?

A unique sensory detail is any detail that answers these four questions:

1. Do the details paint a mental picture for the reader or listener?
2. Do the details involve one of the five senses (sight, smell, taste, touch, and sound)?
3. Does the detail include equivocations?
4. Would the writer or speaker include these details if fabricating the story?

Compare the following two statements and ask the above questions to determine which contains unique sensory details.

"I believe he had a knife."

or

"The handle of the knife was wrapped with black electrical tape. I could feel the rough edge when he rubbed it on my neck."

Which statement paints a mental picture?

Obviously, the second statement does.

Which statement involves one of the five senses?

Again, the second statement does.

Does the detail include an equivocation? Yes. The victim in the first statement uses the equivocation of "I believe" concerning whether the assailant even had a weapon. We are left wondering if there was even a weapon present. If you are assailed by someone with a knife, you will know it and not have to equivocate about that detail. According to Dr. Susan Adams, unique sensory details should not include any equivocation.

If someone was lying about being assaulted by a knife-wielding maniac, would the person give all the details in the second statement, or would they keep it generic like the first statement?

If they were lying, they would stick with the first, because it is easier to remember and they are not likely to be tripped up when questioned because their statement gives almost no pertinent information.

The Five Senses

Some examples of how unique sensory details relate to the five senses are:

- Sight— "I looked back and saw flames shooting out the windows of the house," versus "I saw the house was on fire."
- Sound—"It sounded like a loud cherry bomb went off" versus "It sounded loud."
- Touch/Feeling— "I could feel searing heat on my face and neck" versus "It was really hot."
- Smell— "He had a strong odor of gasoline" versus "I think he smelled bad."
- Taste— "It tasted like bitter Mountain Dew" versus "It sorta tasted bad."

Each of these examples paints a descriptive picture and uses one of the five senses.

Spatial Details

A spatial detail is any location given in a statement that is specific enough that one can go there and find forensic evidence. For example, if someone notifies the police that they were robbed while on campus at a local college, that is not detailed enough to conduct any type of productive investigation. If the victim advises that they were robbed in the student union building, it is getting closer and more detailed, but still too general to be considered a spatial detail. If the victim then advises that he was robbed inside the first-floor men's bathroom while standing at the middle sink washing his hands, now we have information specific enough to be considered a spatial detail.

Once again, when being deceptive, one will not want to give precise spatial detail because there may be security cameras in the area to disprove their story or witnesses to show that they weren't at the location. Keeping it non-specific is always safer.

Details

Let's look at a statement for details and emotions.

Remember, we are looking for unique sensory details, spatial details, and if and where emotions show up in a statement.

Warning: This statement contains explicit language.

The first statement involves a sexual assault that occurred in a small movie theater in Bonnie Lake, Washington.

I was at Bonnie Lake movie theater and halfway through the movie I got up to go to the restroom and walked into the restroom and went to the end install and was about to turn around and shut the door when a man about 19 or 20 turned me around and slammed me into the wall and locked the door. I was about to yell, and he put his hand over my mouth and said "don't talk or I will beat the shit out of you." I still tried to scream but he slapped me in the face and said not to make a noise or he'd beat the shit out of me, grabbing me by shirt and shoulders too. He then undid my pants (struggling) I tried to not let him, but he got them off of one leg. He then undid his pants and took them down only a little way. He had a condom on already and it was orange. He braced his right arm up against the wall and put his penis in me. I was against the wall straddling the toilet and he was doing the same facing me. His left hand was behind my right leg and he had sex with me. It wasn't for very long and when he was done, he pulled up his pants and I was crying, and he pushed me and left the restroom. I was in shock shock and I just sat there. I didn't know what to do. He had a white shirt with the logo on the front. Blue jeans too. He had a crooked tooth, short dirty blonde spiked hair and was shorter than me (5'9"). He had a dark leather bracelet on one hand. I was wearing Express Jeans, flip-flops, and a T-shirt. I didn't tell anyone except Sophia Yost.

What are the unique sensory details and spatial details in this statement?

When reading the statement, the first detail is in line three, where she states she went into the "end stall" in the bathroom. This is a spatial detail. A spatial detail is any location that is specific enough that one can go there and find forensic evidence. If she said she was assaulted in the movie theater, that is too non-specific to be of much use. If she said she was assaulted in the women's bathroom, it is becoming more specific but not enough for it to be considered a spatial detail. By placing the assault location as the "end stall," she has made the detail so specific that anyone can go there and obtain evidence if there is any.

The next detail is in line four, where it is stated the man, "turned me around and slammed me into the wall." This is a unique sensory detail. It addresses sense of touch and it paints a mental picture of what was happening in the "end stall" with no equivocation.

The next unique sensory detail is in line 5 where she states, "he put his hand over my mouth and said, 'don't talk or I will beat the shit out of you.' I still tried to scream but he slapped me in the face and said not to make a noise or he'd beat the shit out of me, grabbing me by shirt and shoulders too." This addresses the senses of touch and sound. Once again, there is no equivocation.

The phrase "grabbing me by shirt and shoulders too" is not only specific regarding sense of touch and paints a mental picture, it is also an unusual way of explaining what happened. It would be much easier to remember that she was just grabbed by the rapist instead of the more detailed "grabbing me by shirt and shoulders too." If I was questioning the victim, I would ask her to show me how she was grabbed by the "shirt and shoulders too." I would want to see if she could keep her story straight over a sustained period of time.

The next unique sensory detail starts in line nine and ends in line fourteen. It is: "He then undid my pants (struggling) I tried to not let him but he got them off of one leg. He then undid his pants and took them down only a little way. He had a condom on already and it was orange. He braced his right arm up against the wall and put his penis in me. I was against the wall straddling the toilet and he was doing the same facing me. His left hand was behind my right leg and he had sex with me."

The detail of the orange condom is obvious, but the other detail that the rapist took her pants off only one leg is unique. It would be much cleaner to say he took my pants off, but she gave the detail that he only got them off one leg. Also, her explanation of the rapist positioning of his and her body during the rape is very detailed.

The last set of unique sensory details starts in line eighteen and ends in line twenty-one. It is: "He had a crooked tooth, short dirty blonde spiked hair and was shorter than me (5'9"). He had a dark leather bracelet on one hand. I was wearing Express jeans, flip-flops, and a T-shirt." This addresses the sense of sight with no equivocation.

Did she express any emotion in the statement and, if she did, where did it appear?

In line sixteen, she stated, "I was in shock, shock." This appeared in the epilogue of the statement, which is where it should appear in a truthful statement.

So, do these details paint a picture in the reader's mind? I believe so. It does in my mind.

Do the details involve any of the five senses? Yes, sight, sound, and touch.

Is there any equivocation? No.

If the victim were making up this story, would she include all these details? Very doubtful.

The level of detail in this statement would be extremely difficult to recall without it being placed in her working and then long-term memory. If someone is fabricating a story such as this, the level of detail would be much less, making it far easier to remember. As stated many times before, lying is hard to do and we usually keep the lie very bare bones so it is easier to remember.

Based on the number of indicators of veracity, I would deem this statement to be credible.

Now, let's look at another sexual assault statement with very few indicators of veracity.

I entered my home through *the back door* to retrieve some items. I was approached from behind. When I turned around, I was faced with someone. *I was hit on the right front of my forehead with a hand.* I was then carried to the upstairs of my home. I was thrown on the bed, held down and cut about my body with what appeared to be a razor, box cutter type thing. Some clothing items were cut off others were pulled off. I struggled, yelled. I broke loose, hit the person with the chair, dazed the person for a second. The person threw me back onto the bed. I then rolled to the floor. I was in and out. I woke, call for help. Person was masked, dark clothing, gloved. Seemed to be male. Tall. Medium build. Did not speak.

There is only one unique sensory detail and one spatial detail in the statement.

"I entered my home through the back door" is a spatial detail.

"I was hit on the right front of my forehead with a hand" addresses the sense of touch.

There is very little detail in this statement.

Where was the victim taken in the upstairs of the house? Was it the victim's bedroom or another bedroom?

The victim states "cut about my body with what appeared to be a razor, box cutter type thing." What part of the victim's body was cut?

The writer uses the equivocation "what appeared to be" to describe the weapon. The victim couldn't give a specific description of the weapon. Was it a box cutter, a razor, or a knife?

"Some clothing items were cut off, others were pulled off." What clothing items were cut off and what items pulled off? Once again, "Some clothing" is an equivocation.

The victim's description of the assailant is so general that it is practically useless.

So let's apply the four unique sensory details questions:

1.   Does this statement paint a mental picture? Hardly
2.   Do any of the details involve the five senses? Marginally
3.   Did the details contain equivocations? Yes
4.   If the person was making up the story, would these details be included in the story? Probably. The details are so sparse, remembering the story would be easy.

Does this sound like a fabricated story, with its lack of unique sensory details, spatial details, and emotions? It does to me.

Let's look at another statement and see if there are any indicators of veracity in the incident box of the statement.

Warning: This statement contained adult language.

I just finished work at the hospital and was walking home to my apartment on the same side of the street. It was a clear, cool night – a nice night for walking. Suddenly someone's ***hand grabbed my throat*** and pulled me into an alley next my apartment building. I tried yelling but he put his hand to my throat. I thought I'd be strangled. He ***tightened his hand so hard around my throat it hurt so bad.*** I couldn't do anything. I just want to live so I did what he demanded. He **pulled a sweater over my head** so I could not see his face. All I could **smell was a strong odor of gasoline or oil**. He told me to take off my clothes. I just couldn't do it, so **he ripped them off**. He got so angry... **I had my period and the tampon was in place and he kept getting angry and pushing my legs up by my head. It was so painful.** When he finally finished raping me, he told me to turn over. **I was so scared.** I didn't know what he was going to do. He asked me to turnover so he could run away without me seeing him. **I just got hysterical** after he left. I'm usually pretty cool and levelheaded, but **I just went to pieces**. I ran out into the street. It's a mainstream but no one stopped, and I was running around. Finally, a car stopped, found out what happened, and the 2 men brought me to the hospital.

As you may recall, all statements can be broken down into three parts: the prologue, everything leading up to the incident; the incident, what happened; and the epilogue, everything that happened after the incident (PIE). A balanced statement would consist a short prologue and a short epilogue, and the bulk of the statement should consist of the incident box.

This statement is fourteen lines long.

The prologue is lines one through three: = 2 ÷ 14 = 14%

The incident box is lines four through fifteen = 9 ÷ 14 = 64%

The epilogue is lines sixteen through nineteen = 3 ÷ 14 = 22%

Based on the PIE calculation, this statement is balanced.

So, within the incident box, are there any indicators of veracity?

Several!

"A hand grabbed my throat, he put his hand to my throat" and "tightened his hand so hard around my throat it hurt so bad" are unique sensory details regarding touch or feeling.

He "pulled a sweater over my head" paints a mental picture.

"All I could smell was a strong odor of gasoline or oil" is a unique sensory detail regarding smell.

"I had my period and the tampon was in place" is a detail that if the victim were making this story up she would most likely not include it due to embarrassment and its personal nature.

"...pushing my legs up by my head. It was so painful" paints a mental picture and deals with touch and feelings.

"I was so scared," "I just got hysterical after he left," and "I just went to pieces" are the emotional responses to the rape, but all of them occur in the epilogue of the statement where they are the most appropriate.

None of the unique sensory details contains equivocations.

There are some spatial details, but they're not great. According to the statement, the rape occurred in an alley next to her building. Which alley is not specified, but that would be easily cleared up in the interview.

Based on the amount and type of unique sensory details in the statement incident, I would deem this statement to be credible.

Finally, let's analyze a statement by someone you all will probably know, George Zimmerman.

George Zimmerman Statement

On the evening of February 26, 2012, George Zimmerman saw a suspicious lone male walking in the rain and looking into the windows of homes located in the community known as The Retreat at Twin Lakes in Sanford, Florida. Zimmerman was part of the Community Patrol and a bit of a police enthusiast.

While Zimmerman was out of his car and on the phone with a 911 operator, he was approached by Trayvon Martin. A physical altercation ensued between the two men. During the altercation, Zimmerman pulled the pistol he was carrying that night and shot and killed Martin.

Zimmerman was taken into custody by the Sanford Police and questioned for five hours. He was then released because, according to Sanford Police Chief Bill Lee and Florida State Attorney Norm Wolfinger, there was no evidence to refute Zimmerman's claims of self-defense. His head injuries were consistent with his story.

The Zimmerman/Martin story took the nation by storm. The news coverage was intense, and much of it misleading. The story became about racial profiling, gun control, and Florida's Stand Your Ground law. President Barack Obama even weighed in on the controversy. Due to the withering news coverage of the case, Florida Governor Rick Scott gave in to political pressure and appointed a Special Prosecutor, Angela Corey, to investigate the case.

On April 11, 2012, Corey charged Zimmerman with murder in the second degree.

On July 13, 2013, a jury acquitted Zimmerman of second-degree murder and the lesser crime of manslaughter.

George Zimmerman may have prevailed in the courts, but his life was ruined.

This is the statement that George Zimmerman gave after shooting Trayvon Martin. While reading it, try to determine if the statement is balanced or unbalanced. Also identify any indicators of veracity, that is, unique sensory details, spatial details, and emotion.

George Zimmerman's statement dated 02/26/2012

1.   In August of 2011 my neighbor's house was broken into while
2.   she was home with her infant son. The intruders attempted to attack
3.   her and her child; however, SPD reported to the scene of the crime
4.   and the robbers fled, my wife saw the intruders running from the
5.   home and became scared of the rising crime within our neighbor-
      hood.

6. I, and my neighbors formed a "Neighborhood Watch Program." We

7. were instructed by SPD to call the non-emergency line if we

8. saw anything suspicious or 911 if we saw a crime in progress.

9. Tonight, I was on my way to the grocery store when I saw

10. a male approximately 5'11" to 6'2" casually walking in the

11. rain looking into homes. I pulled my vehicle over and called

12. SPD non-emergency phone number. I told the dispatcher

13. what I had witnessed, the dispatcher took

14. note of my location + the suspect fled

15. to a darkened area of the sidewalk as the dispatcher was

16. asking me for an exact location the suspect emerged from

17. the darkness + circled my vehicle. I could not hear if he

18. said anything. The suspect once again disappeared between the

19. back of some houses. The dispatcher once again asked me for

20. my exact location. I could not remember the name of the street

21. so, I got out of my car to look for a street sign. The dispatcher

22. asked me for a description and the direction the suspect went.

23. I told the dispatcher I did not know but I was out of my

24. vehicle looking for a street sign + the direction the suspect was.

25. The dispatcher told me not to follow the suspect + that an officer

26. was in route. As I headed back to my vehicle the

27. suspect emerged from the darkness and

28. said "you got a problem" I said "no"

29. The suspect said, "you do now." As I looked

30. and tried to find my phone to dial 911 the suspect punched

31. me in the face. I fell backwards onto my back. The

32. suspect got on top of me. I yelled "Help" several times

33. The suspect told me "shut the fuck up" as I tried to sit up

34. right, the suspect grabbed my head and slammed it into

35. the concrete sidewalk several times. I continued to yell "Help"

36. each time I attempted to sit up, the suspect slammed my head

37. into the sidewalk. My head felt like it was going to explode.

38. I tried to slide out from under the suspect and continue

39. to yell "Help." As I slid, the suspect covered my mouth

40. and nose and stopped my breathing. At this point I felt

41. the suspect reach for my now exposed firearm and say

42. "Your gonna die tonight Mother Fucker." I

43. unholstered my firearm in fear for my

44. life as he had assured me, he was going to kill

45. me and fired one shot into his torso. The suspect

46. sat back allowing me to sit up and said "You got me"

47. At this point I slid out from underneath him and

48. got on top of the suspect holding his hands away from

49. his body. An onlooker appeared and asked me if I was ok

50. I said "no" he said, "I am calling 911." I said I don't

51. need you to call 911. " I already called them I need you to

52. help me restrain this guy." At this point an SPD officer

53. arrived and asked, "who shot him" I said, "I did" and

54. I placed my hands on top of my head and told the officer

55. where on my person my firearm was holstered. The

56. officer handcuffed me and disarmed me. The officer

57. then placed me in the back of his vehicle.

Let's calculate the PIE.

The statement is 57 lines long.

The Prologue is 25 lines long – 25 ÷ 57 = 44%

The Incident Box is 27 lines long – 27 ÷ 57 = 47%

The Epilogue is 5 lines long – 5 ÷ 57 = 9%

Based on the PIE calculation, the statement is balanced.

So, within the Incident box are there any Unique Sensory Details?

Line 32 - "The suspect got on top of me."

Line 34-35 - "the suspect grabbed my head and slammed it into the concrete sidewalk"

Line 36-37 - "each time I attempted to sit up, the suspect slammed my head into the sidewalk. My head felt like it was going to explode."

Line 38 - "I tried to slide out from under the suspect"

Line 39-40 - "As I slid, the suspect covered my mouth and nose and stopped my breathing."

Line 47-49- "I slid out from underneath him and got on top of the suspect holding his hands away from me."

The statement contains numerous unique sensory details in the incident box. They paint a mental picture of what was occurring between Zimmerman and Martin, involves the five senses, contains no equivocations, and probably would not be included if Zimmerman was fabricating the story due to the head injuries needed to support a fabricated violent encounter.

Remember, statements that contain unique sensory details, spatial details, and emotions, in the right part of the statement, are usually truthful.

This chapter started with the testimony of an elderly woman known as Miss Hattie who fought back when a man entered her home with the intention of raping her.

Go back and re-read her testimony with an eye for the unique sensory details and spatial details. It is chock full of them!

Miss Hattie gives a vivid description of her assailant, what he did and said, and how she handled the situation. She paints a mental picture of her struggle with the assailant. Her statement's unique sensory details involve the sense of touch and sound. She makes it pretty clear that she wasn't holding the would-be rapist's hand, that's for sure!

She uses good spatial details to tell where the assault happened.

Every time I read her testimony, I smile. Thank god there are people like Miss Hattie, a tough ol' gal who just wasn't going to be a victim.

Quick Tips

1. Unique sensory details involve one or more of the five senses: sight, sound, touch, smell, and taste.

2. Unique sensory details answer the following questions:

    - Does the detail involve one of the five senses?

    - Do the details paint a mental picture?

    - Does the detail contain any equivocations?

    - If the details were fabricated or made up, would the speaker/writer include the details?

3. Spatial details involve very specific locations.

CHAPTER 5:
Emotions

Emotions play an important role in everyone's life.

Imagine a life where you had no emotions. No joy or sadness. No highs or lows. Never experiencing the exhilaration of achievement or the feeling of disappointment when you come up short and the feeling of determination to get it right next time. Just flat. That would make for a miserable existence.

Even fear, when thought of in the right context, is something we should welcome. In his book, *The Gift of Fear: Survival Signals That Protect Us from Violence*, author Gavin de Becker advises that fear informs us when danger is near even if we don't recognize it. People seldom listen to the little voice in the back of their mind that tells them that something is wrong, whether it is someone who just creeps them out or when someone is telling them something that just feels false. A large part of the mission of this book is get people to listen to their inner voice when they think they're being deceived and to recognize when their inner voice is warning them to beware.

Emotions are involuntary and universal. They are universal because everyone has them and involuntary because no one can stop emotions.

How people display them, well, is a different matter.

We have all seen people who display calm when in a stressful situation. We refer to them as having nerves of steel, as having ice water in their veins, or as someone who is emotionless. The reality is that Liam Neeson seemed completely in control in the movie *Taken*, but his emotions were running high. Otherwise, he wouldn't have done what was necessary to rescue his daughter. He just didn't display them until he had safely rescued her. That is when he showed emotion.

Emotions are universal because all people, regardless of age, race, and gender have the same emotions. We all experience happiness and joy. We all laugh and smile. We all become angry sometimes and are fearful on occasion. A Pacific Islander feels happiness in the same way that a German in Dusseldorf does. A Brooklyn steel worker feels sadness and disappointment the same as a South African businessman.

Paul Eckman, author of *Emotions Revealed: Recognizing Faces and Feelings to Improve Communications and Emotional Life* breaks emotions down into the following categories:

1. Fear
2. Anger
3. Sadness
4. Happiness
5. Contempt
6. Surprise
7. Disgust

A study published in the *Journal of Experimental Psychology* revealed that "the recall of experienced events includes more affective information, such as emotional reactions, than does recall of created events." (M.K. Johnson, M.A. Foley, A.G. Suengas, & C.L. Raye, "Phenomenal characteristics of memories for perceived and imaged autobiographical events," *Journal of Experimental Psychology*, 1988, 117(4))

According to Arne Trankell in *Reliability of Evidence: Methods for Analyzing and Assessing Witness Statements*, (Stockholm Sweden, Rotobeckman, 1972),

"Emotional experiences were found to be present in truthful witness accounts but not generally in constructed ones."

So, studies show that emotions are often found in truthful statements, but when should they appear?

According to research, emotions typically show up in the epilogue of the statement, especially when recalling a traumatic event.

Personally, after looking at hundreds and hundreds of statements, my experience has been that emotions, if they show up at all, show up in the epilogue or late in the incident box of truthful statements. Statements where emotions show up in the prologue or early in the incident box raise a red flag to me. I will always take note of that for further questioning.

You may not agree with me but consider this: recall a time you almost got into an auto accident or something which could have resulted in grievous bodily harm or death. When did you experience fear or relief? During the incident or after?

Let me tell you a story.

In 1992, I lived in eastern New Mexico and taught Army ROTC at Eastern New Mexico University in Portales, New Mexico, a town at the time of probably 15,000. This is ranch county, with wide-open spaces and little traffic. It's a perfect place to ride motorcycles.

One afternoon, I was riding my motorcycle home after work when a young lady made a left turn to enter the university and ran into me. I didn't see her, and she didn't see me. We collided, my bike striking her left front fender. All I remember thinking was, *Oh shit*, and then, bam!

I recall seeing yellow (the color of her car), blue sky, and black asphalt, in that order. I then remember rolling down the street like a ball. A witness to the event later stated that I did a somersault over the car and landed on my feet and then rolled down the street for approximately twenty feet.

So, I'm lying in the street thinking to myself, *I hope I'm not paralyzed*. I turned my head to the right and the left. So far, so good! Then I sat up. *Okay, I'm not paralyzed*. Then my feet started hurting like someone had taken a baseball bat and beaten the bottoms of my feet. I really didn't know why they were hurting until I found out later that I had landed on my feet after the somersault over the car.

Eventually, the ambulance came and took me to the hospital. I broke a couple of bones in my right foot, but that was all. The young lady had a small cut on her head and my bike was totaled. (When I involuntarily braced myself before the collision, my legs tightened up to the point of crushing the bike's gas tank upon impact.)

All through this, I didn't experience any strong emotions except a little relief. It wasn't until I got home and was watching Monday Night Football with my youngest son, Tyson, that I really got emotional. I looked at Tyson, and I remembered all the times I had taken him for rides with me and I realized how unnecessarily I had put him in danger. That is when I got emotional. I actually got scared.

Why didn't I experience emotions earlier? I think it has to do with the fight or flight experience. When in the middle of a traumatic experience, you really don't have the time or luxury to emote. You are just trying to survive. You'll have time for emotions after you have survived, and if you don't survive, well, it won't make much of a difference, will it?

Go back to the Susan Smith statement and you'll see that she introduces emotions very early in the prologue and she keeps bringing them up throughout the statement. Why did she do that? Why did she find it necessary to let the reader know that she was upset and had been crying? Was she upset about her deteriorating relationship with Tom or what she was about to do to her two young sons?

Oscar Pistorius Statement

South African Paralympic sprinter Oscar Pistorius, aka the Blade Runner, burst onto the sports scene in August 2012 when he became the first amputee runner to compete at both the Olympic Games and the Paralympics. Pistorius was the darling of the media. His story was compelling due to his extreme physical disadvantages. He seemed like a man who had faced adversity and had overcome it. But as we all know, things aren't always what they seem.

Outside the sporting arena, Pistorius had a checkered past. He had a history of domestic violence and alcohol abuse.

In February 2013, Pistorius was dating South African model Reeve Steenkamp. On the night before Valentine's Day, Pistorius and Steenkamp spent a quiet evening at home. Sometime in the night, Pistorius shot Steenkamp four times with his 9 mm Parabellum pistol, thinking she was an intruder in his home.

The following is the statement Pistorius gave the court in his defense. Emotions show up in the statement in places that make it questionable. The identified emotions are highlighted.

Oscar Pistorius Statement

"On the 13th of February, Reeva would have gone out with her friends and I with my friends. Reeva then called me and asked that if we rather spend the evening at home. I agreed and we were content to have a quiet dinner together at home. By 2200 on 13 February 2013 we were in our bedroom. She was doing her yoga exercises and I was in bed watching television. My prosthetic legs were off. We were ***deeply in love*** and ***I could not be happier***. I know she felt the same way. She had given me a present for Valentine's Day but asked me only to open it the next day.

After Reeva finished her yoga exercises, she got in bed and we both fell asleep. I am acutely aware of violent crime being committed by intruders entering homes with a view to commit crime, including violent crime. I have received death threats before. I have also been a victim of violence and of burglaries before. For that reason, I kept a firearm, a 9mm Parabellum, underneath my bed when I went to bed at night.

During the early morning hours of 14 February 2013, I woke up, went onto the balcony to bring the fan in and closed the sliding doors, the blinds and the curtains. I heard a noise in the bathroom and realized that someone was in the bathroom.

I felt a **sense of terror** rushing over me. There are no burglar bars across the bathroom window, and I knew that contractors who worked at my house had left the ladders outside. Although I did not have my prosthetic legs on, I have mobility on my stumps. I believe that someone had entered my house. I was **too scared** to switch a light on.

I grabbed my 9mm pistol from underneath my bed. On my way to the bathroom I screamed words to the effect for him/them to get out of my house and for Reeva to phone the police. It was pitch dark in the bedroom and I thought Reeva was in bed.

I noticed that the bathroom window was open. I realized that the intruder/s was/were in the toilet because the toilet door was closed, and I did not see anyone in the bathroom. I heard movement inside the toilet. The toilet is inside the bathroom and has a separate door.

It filled me with **horror and fear** of an intruder or intruders being inside the toilet. I thought he or they must have entered through the unprotected window. As I did not have my prosthetic legs on and felt **extremely vulnerable**. I knew I had to protect Reeva and myself. I believed that when the intruder/s came out of the toilet we would be in grave danger. I felt trapped as my bedroom door was locked and I have limited mobility only on stumps.

I fired shots at the toilet door and shouted to Reeva to phone the police. She did not respond, and I moved backwards out of my bathroom, keeping my eyes on the bathroom entrance. Everything was pitch dark in the bedroom and I was still ***too scare***d to switch on a light. Reeva was not responding. When I reached the bed, I realized that Reeva was not in bed. That is when it dawned on me it could have been Reeva who was in the toilet. I returned to the bathroom calling her name. I tried to open the toilet door, but it was locked. I rushed back into the bedroom and opened the sliding door exiting onto the balcony and screamed for help.

I put on my prosthetic legs, ran back to the bathroom and tried to kick the toilet door open. I think I must then have turned on the lights. I went back into bedroom and grabbed my cricket bat to bash open the door. A panel or panels broke off and I found the key on the floor and unlocked and opened the toilet door. Reeva was slumped over but alive.

I battled to get her out of the toilet and pulled her into the bathroom. I phoned Johan Stander who was involved in the administration of the estate and asked him to phone the ambulance. I phoned Netcare and asked for help. I went downstairs to open the front door. I returned to the bathroom and picked Reeva up as I had been told not to wait for the paramedics, but to take her to the hospital. I carried her downstairs in order to take her to the hospital. On the way down, Stander arrived. A doctor who lives in the complex also arrived. Downstairs, I tried to render the assistance to Reeva that I could, but she died in my arms.

I am absolutely ***mortified*** by the events and the devastating loss of my beloved Reeva. With the benefit of hindsight, I believe that Reeva went to the toilet when I went out on my balcony to bring the fan in. I cannot bear to think of the suffering I have caused her and her family, knowing how much she was loved. I also know that the events of that tragic night were as I have described them and that in due course, I have no doubt the police and expert investigators will bear this out."

As always, calculate the PIE.

The statement is 54 lines long.

The Prologue is 13 lines long = 13 ÷ 54 = 24%

The Incident Box is 20 lines long= 20 ÷ 54 = 37%

The Epilogue is 21 lines long = 21 ÷ 54 = 39%

The statement is slightly out of balance with Epilogue being too long. This is indicative of trying to justify the actions taken during the Incident. Pistorius is attempting to convince more than convey information.

Emotions show up early and often in Pistorius's statement. The problem is where the emotion occurs. The majority of the references to emotion occurred in the prologue and incident box. Almost all of the emotions involve fear and terror. The only emotion in the epilogue is when he says he is "mortified" by the events and the loss of Steenkamp.

Pistorius was a world-class athlete. He was an athlete his entire life, participating in rugby, water polo, and Olympic wrestling despite having his legs amputated as an infant due to Fibular Hemimelia (congenital absence of the fibula) in both legs. And as with most athletes, Pistorius thought of himself as a man's man, a tough guy like most jocks. If you ever ask a jock if they were scared, no matter the incident, they will almost always deny it. But according to Pistorius's account, as soon as he heard a bump in the night, he was in terror and too scared to turn on a light despite being armed. He later says he was "filled with horror and fear" and was "extremely vulnerable." Pistorius says he felt in grave danger and trapped. I don't know. Call me jaded, but it sounds like he is trying to convince the court that he was in mortal danger and so afraid that he accidentally shot Steenkamp.

In September 2014, Pistorius was convicted of culpable homicide and received a prison sentenced of five years. This sentence was appealed by the prosecutors, who argued that the sentence was too lenient considering the crime. The appellant court agreed and in 2017 increased Pistorius's sentence to thirteen years.

There are other aspects of this statement that jump out to me. One of those aspects is the use of extraneous information in Pistorius's statement. The next chapter will delve more deeply into extraneous information and how it is used to deceive.

Quick Tips

1. Emotions are involuntary and universal.

2. Emotions often are present in truthful statements.

3. In truthful statements, emotions will occur in the epilogue portion of the statement or late in the incident portion.

4. If emotions show up in the prologue or throughout the statement, the statement may be suspect.

CHAPTER 6:

Extraneous Information

If you have ever watched a magician, you have witnessed the art of misdirection. The magician deftly misdirects your attention so you don't notice how he cups the card in his hand. You don't see what he is really doing because you are busy looking at something else.

That's what extraneous information is, misdirection. When Susan Smith gives pages of information while not answering the basic question of what happened when her children were kidnapped, she is diverting your attention away from what is important and misdirecting it to the unimportant. And she is hoping you won't notice that she is not being helpful in finding her children.

When people deceive many use extraneous information as their go-to technique. They want to muddy the waters to hide the lie they are about to tell. They answer questions that were never asked. Smith used extraneous information to reveal what she fed her children, that Tom Findlay and Susan Brown were on a date at Hickory Nuts, and that she talked to her estranged husband. But the question she needed to answer was, "What happened during the carjacking and kidnapping of your children?" It took her seventy-eight lines to get to the point where she answers that question.

Extraneous information is used for two primary reasons.

The first reason is to justify actions and behaviors. Smith uses extraneous information about taking the kids for a drive to justify why she was at the traffic light in Union, South Carolina, where the alleged carjacking took place. As you will recall, Smith claimed to be upset and decided to go her mother's house and then changed her mind and decided to go to see Mitch, a friend of Smith's. She needed to be in her car for the carjacking to occur and she needed the carjacking to occur in order to end up on foot at the John D. Long Lake where she rolled her red Mazda into the lake, drowning her two sons. So, when we reread the extraneous information in the prologue of her statement, it becomes plain that she needed to set the stage for her behaviors. There is always a reason why extraneous information is used in a statement. In Smith's case, it didn't happen by accident.

Second, extraneous information is used to buy time. As stated before, lying by commission is hard to do, even for hardened criminals. So extraneous information is used to buy time before telling The Lie. Smith certainly used it in her statement. Additionally, extraneous information can misdirect the reader or listener to believe that the person giving the statement is being cooperative and is providing a lot of details. The problem is that the details are of minimal value and don't answer the important question or address the main topic.

A good example of using extraneous information to buy time before lying by commission is an interview of Paul Bernardo, aka the Scarborough Rapist. Bernardo was a serial rapist operating in Scarborough, Ontario, Canada. It is unknown how many rape victims Bernardo has under his belt, but he was convicted in 1993 for the rape of at least a dozen of women and the murders of four young girls. In a strange twist, his wife, Karla Homolka, assisted Bernardo in the murders and sexual assaults. In an even stranger turn of events, one of Bernardo's and Homolka's victims was Tammy Lyn Homolka, Homolka's little sister.

Go to YouTube, and search, "Paul Bernardo, did you kill Elizabeth Bain?" There you will see an interview of Bernardo by Canadian law enforcement. At the beginning of the video, Bernardo is asked, "Did you kill Elizabeth Bain?" Bernardo talks nonstop for a minute and forty seconds, not answering the question. At the two minutes and two seconds mark, he finally answers and says that he did not kill Elizabeth Bain. He was buying time before telling the lie that he did not kill her.

Extraneous information is anything that doesn't answer the question asked. Therefore, it is important when asking for a statement to be always very specific about what you are asking for. If you ask for the writer to "Tell me what happened," that gives them permission to wander as far afield as they wish. If you say, "Tell me about the robbery," now they know specifically you are asking for. If they give you a lot of extraneous information and minimal information concerning the incident, they are using deceptive language.

Extraneous information is used to give the impression that the writer is being cooperative and very forthcoming. The writer gives a lot of detail leading up to the incident to show that they aren't hiding anything. But what is the quality of the details they are providing?

Let's look at the statement from Chapter 3, Balance vs Unbalanced Statements, with a lot of extraneous information.

When the wake-up call came at 6 AM, I was already up because I don't sleep well in motels. I had been watching early news; they were talking about the terrible airline crash; they are still finding body parts. I then took a shower (it was a quick one because the water was not very hot), got dressed and went to the lobby for their continental breakfast. I had a doughnut (greasy but good) and a cup of coffee. I then went back to my room, checked to make sure I had packed everything, got my bags, and put them in the trunk of the car. I then went back to the lobby to check out. I got another cup of coffee while I was there. I then used my Visa card to pay for the room, but the system was down and it took some time to verify it. I then walked to my car and as I was putting my key in the lock a man poked something in my back and told me not to move. He took my keys and my wallet and told me to get in the car and lie face down and not move. I did as I was told until I was sure he was gone. I then went back to the lobby and had them call 911 and waited for you to get here.

Everything before the robbery (incident) is extraneous information. It's easy to see how out of balance the statement is. The majority of the statement is in the prologue leading up to the actual robbery and it is all extraneous information.

In this statement, the writer told us about his state of sleep in the hotel, his shower, what he had for breakfast, packing his belongings, and paying for his night's stay. In a 13-line statement, the writer spent the first nine lines talking about everything except the subject of the statement, to wit, the robbery. He only dedicated two lines to talking about the most significant thing that probably happened to him in his life. But it was only given two lines. Does that pass the common-sense test? Let me answer that. No!

The fact is the writer of this statement was being deceptive. It turns out that the writer was a traveling salesman who engaged in a bit of commerce with a lady of the night (a soiled dove, if you will), who stole his money out of his wallet while he was in the bathroom. He created the robbery story to explain how he lost all his money but not his wallet (the police found his wallet with all his credit cards and driver's license in the bushes beside the parking lot where he had tossed it). He used extraneous information to justify his actions and behaviors and to also buy time before telling The Lie.

Here is a fun little statement. Try to determine where the extraneous information is located in the statement.

"Why was that woman in our car?"

After work, I dropped into Damon's to catch the Redskins on TV. There was a lady sitting next to me and we chatted briefly. The Redskins were down 14-6 at halftime and we knew that both the Skins and the Cowboys needed this one. The Cowboys kicked off to start the second half and we ran it back for a touchdown. The crowd was going nuts. Then the Cowboys fumbled on their next possession and the Skins returned it for another score. People were high-fiving each other and everyone was buying rounds of beer. I drank slowly because I knew I had to drive home. I even ate a burger. After that, the woman who had been sitting next to me asked me for a ride and so I gave her one.

This statement is ten lines long, and eight of the ten lines consist of extraneous information.

"Why was that woman in our car?"

After work, I dropped into Damon's to catch the Redskins on TV. *There was a lady sitting next to me and we chatted briefly. The Redskins were down 14-6 at halftime and we knew that both the Skins and the Cowboys needed this one. The Cowboys kicked off to start the second half and we ran it back for a touchdown. The crowd was going nuts. Then the Cowboys fumbled on their next possession and the Skins returned it for another score. People were high-fiving each other and everyone was buying rounds of beer. I drank slowly because I knew I had to drive home. I even ate a burger.* After that, the woman who had been sitting next to me

The husband isn't answering the questions asked. He uses extraneous information to buy time and justify his actions, such as giving the woman a ride (awkward!).

Literally every line except the first and last one in this statement is extraneous information.

But don't be fooled in to thinking extraneous information is not important. Some very important details are sometimes hidden in the extraneous information.

Take a look at the following statement regarding the arson of a house that was under construction. See if you can pick out the one line of extraneous information in the statement.

"Well the day before the fire all of us showed up to work. All we had left was finishing drywall work that consisted of mudding taping and sanding. Berry took Sam & Sam to start another job and left Van and I.

We took are (sic) time because we wanted to do a good job. I had been bringing my fishing pole and fishing on my breaks. We worked pretty hard all day and thought we did a good day's work. Berry came back at the end of the day bitching like he was in a bad mood and said we did get enough done. So, I cleaned up and left.

When I came to work the next morning the Fire Dept. was there. I called my Bud over who is a fireman and he said the house burned in the night,"

Well The day Before The FiRe
alloF us showed up To work. all we
had left was finishing dRywall work
that consisT of mudding Taping and
Sanding. BeRRy Took Sam & Sam To STaRT
another Job and LefT Van and I.

We TooK are Time Because
we wanTed To do a good Job.
I had Been BRing my fishing pole
and fishing on my Breaks. we worked
pretty had all day and ThoughT we did
a good days work. BeRRy came at The
end of The day Ditching like he was
in a Bad mood and said we did geT
enough done, so I cleaned up and
left.

When I came To work
The nexT morning The FiRe Dept. was
There. I called my Bud over who is a
FiReman, and he said The house Burned
in The night.

Did you find the extraneous information?

It is located in the second paragraph. It is, "I had been bringing my fishing pole and fishing on my breaks." He is giving a statement about a house he was building burning down overnight, so why is "bringing my fishing pole and fishing on my breaks" important enough to be included in his statement? Remember, things included in statements don't happen by accident.

Turns out that the writer and his friend, Van, stole and hid a bunch of his boss's tools and equipment in the nearby woods where there was a small fishing pond. The writer of the statement was actually seen coming out of the woods by his boss, so he needed a reason to justify why he was in the woods, hence the "fishing on my break". At the end of the day, Van and the writer poured about five gallons of gas in the house and set it on fire to cover the theft.

They both confessed and pled guilty to arson and larceny.

Let's look at one more statement with extraneous information.

Tell us what you know about the robbery.

"I work the 12m to 8a shift at the warehouse. I am the only guard on duty during that shift. I like to arrive at work a few minutes early, usually 10-15 minutes. This gives me time to talk to the guard I relieve.

On the night of the break-in, I arrived at 11:50 pm. Don Smith, the 4p-12m guard, and I had a conversation about the ball game being interrupted by the earthquake. It was a terrible thing to happen, especially for serious baseball fans. We talked about my being a Reds fan and him being a fan the Dodgers. We also talked about the weather here locally and the problems with the economy. Dan left at 11:55 pm since he knows I like to start my rounds at exactly 12:00 midnight.

I began to suspect something was wrong about 3:00 am when I noticed the back gate was unlocked. A few minutes later, I was convinced that something was wrong when I found the payroll office door unlocked and the safe open.

I recalled reading a story last year about money being taken from another warehouse. The guy who took the money wasn't caught. My first reaction was to call the boss. The boss has instructed us to call him in any emergency. He was pretty upset when I woke him at 4:00am. *At no time did I see any strangers in the warehouse that night.* My boss suggested that we add another guard to the night shift. I told him I believe this is a good idea since it might help prevent future thefts. That's basically what happen that night."

The statement is twenty-two lines long. The PIE is as follows:

P = 10÷22 = 45%

I = 4÷22 = 18%

E = 8÷22 = 36%

The statement is out of balance. The robbery information is by far the smallest portion of the statement.

Within the prologue and epilogue of the statement, the writer provides a lot extraneous information. Let's look at the statement again, this time with the extraneous information highlighted.

Tell us what you know about the robbery.

"I work the 12m to 8a shift at the warehouse. I am the only guard on duty during that shift. I like to arrive at work a few minutes early, usually 10-15 minutes. This gives me time to talk to the guard I relieve.

On the night of the break-in, I arrived at 11:50 pm. *Don Smith, the 4p-12m guard, and I had a conversation about the ball game being interrupted by the earthquake. It was a terrible thing to happen, especially for serious baseball fans. We talked about my being a Reds fan and him being a fan the Dodgers. We also talked about the weather here locally and the problems with the economy. Dan left at 11:55 pm since he knows I like to start my rounds at exactly 12:00 midnight.*

I began to suspect something was wrong about 3:00 am when I noticed the back gate was unlocked. A few minutes later, I was convinced that something was wrong when I found the payroll office door unlocked and the safe open.

I recalled reading a story last year about money being taken from another warehouse. The guy who took the money wasn't caught. My first reaction was to call the boss. The boss has instructed us to call him in any emergency. He was pretty upset when I woke him at 4:00am. At no time did I see any strangers in the warehouse that night. *My boss suggested that we add another guard to the night shift. I told him I believe this is a good idea since it might help prevent future thefts. That's basically what happen that night."*

As you can see, most of the statement consists of extraneous information. He is using extraneous information for all of the reasons we've talked about. He is buying time, answering questions never asked, justifying his actions and trying to look like he is being very helpful.

One other thing. Look at this line; At **no time did I see any strangers in the warehouse that night.** Why did he use the term "strangers"? That is what I call an unusual noun. If he didn't see any "strangers", did he see any friends or acquaintances? Sounds like an inside job to me.

The Oscar Pistorius statement from the previous chapter contained the following paragraph that was purely extraneous information.

"After Reeva finished her yoga exercises, she got in bed and we both fell asleep. **I am acutely aware of violent crime being committed by intruders entering homes with a view to commit crime, including violent crime. I have received death threats before. I have also been a victim of violence and of burglaries before. For that reason, I kept a firearm, a 9mm Parabellum, underneath my bed when I went to bed at night."**

Pistorius uses this extraneous information to convey his state of mind and to justify possessing the firearm that was used in the crime.

So, remember, when someone gives way too much extraneous information to a straightforward question, they may be justifying their actions or behaviors, buying time, or misdirecting you into believing they are being very forthcoming while providing few pertinent details.

Quick Tips

1. Extraneous Information is used for several reasons:

    - To justify the speaker/writer's actions.
    - To buy time before telling a lie.
    - To appear to be cooperative while providing little useful information.

2. Do not disregard extraneous information because of its name. Many times, pertinent information may be imbedded in extraneous information.

3. Remember, people always have a reason for including extraneous information. We just have to figure out what that is.

CHAPTER 7:

Waffles Words and Selective Amnesia

One of the most common forms of deception is the use of equivocations and negations.

Equivocation, also known as hedge words, qualifiers, weasel words, or waffle words, can be defined as the use of vague language to hide one's meaning or to avoid committing to a point of view.

Dishonest politicians (are there any other kind?) use equivocation all the time. This allows them to take all sides of an issue without taking a firm stand on anything. In a legal context, equivocations allow someone to avoid admitting guilt while abstaining from telling a bald-faced lie.

Negation is the contradiction or denial of something. Some synonyms for negation are contradiction, repudiation, refuting, and disclaiming. The Latin origin of the word negation is *negatio*, which means "to deny."

The use of equivocations and negations may or may not be appropriate when used in a statement. It really comes down to the context of how they are used and the frequency of use.

Some examples of equivocations are:

- around
- somewhat

- probably
- kind of
- maybe
- something
- someone
- I think
- I believe
- like

Equivocations lack specificity and detail. Statements containing equivocations are much easier to maintain over a long period of time because they lack details and are easier to remember.

After examining a statement and highlighting all of the equivocation, always ask yourself, *Are they appropriate?*. Many times, it just comes down to the context of how they are used.

Examples of negation are:

- not
- no
- didn't
- wouldn't
- nothing
- never

Negations are also used to indicate a lack of knowledge and a lack of memory or as I call it, selective amnesia. An example of a lack of knowledge is "I don't know" or "I'm not sure." A lack of memory would be "I don't remember" or "I can't recall."

A lack of memory is a red flag for me when talking about a significant incident or moment in time. People forget unimportant things such as what you had for lunch two days ago. But if you were robbed outside your house on your way to work two days ago, you would most likely remember that incident in vivid detail.

A lack of memory tells me that you have the memory stored in your hard drive, your brain memory center, and it only needs to be coaxed out. Whereas, a lack of knowledge means you don't have this memory because you have no first-person knowledge of the topic at hand.

For example, I may not be able to remember the name of my first-grade teacher, but I have no knowledge of the name of your first-grade teacher. With enough prompting and memory recall, I may recall the name of my first-grade teacher, but no amount of prompting will give me the knowledge of who your first-grade teacher was.

When someone professes to not remember something they should have knowledge of due to their position or association with a person or incident, I look very closely at that. For example, if your teenager comes home late and you ask them where they went and with who, and their answer is "I don't remember," that's a problem. Why don't they remember? Were they drugged and can't remember? Are they being forced by outside influences not to reveal what they did? Are they trying to protect someone or just trying to avoid getting in trouble for being somewhere they shouldn't have been?

A good example of a selective amnesia is former FBI Director James Comey's congressional testimony regarding the FBI's Crossfires Hurricane investigation, also known as the Russian Collusion investigation.

During Comey's six-hour, closed-door testimony, he used "I don't know" 166 times, "I don't remember" 71 times, and "I can't recall" 8 times. That is 245 times he used these equivocations and negations in a six-hour period. He averaged an "I don't know," "I don't remember," or "I don't recall," every 1 minute and 46 seconds!

Of course some of these questions may have been about items he had no knowledge of, but he claimed to not know who initiated the Crossfire Hurricane investigation or which FBI investigator interviewed Hillary Clinton about her use of a private email server. Let me tell you as a retired FBI agent, I don't believe that for a second. Here's why.

This investigation was so high profile that everyone on the seventh floor of the FBI Headquarters, up to the Director himself, was briefed daily on the status of the investigation. The FBI Director has a meeting that occurs every morning to brief him on the most significant cases the FBI is handling. For Comey to say he didn't know who started the most high-profile investigation in the FBI's history, and certainly during his tenure, or who conducted the most pivotal interview in the investigation one day before he exonerated Hillary Clinton is laughable. He was being purposefully deceptive.

Another red flag for me is when someone is asked a direct question and they answer it by telling me what they didn't or wouldn't do.

For example, if you ask your teenage son if he drove your car without your permission and he answers the question with, "Why would you ask me such a thing? I would never do that," he is being deceptive because he didn't answer your question and he is feebly trying to lay a guilt trip on you for asking such an intrusive question. Explore further!

Let's look at some statements with equivocations and negations.

At a high school, a male teacher was accused of making sexual advances to a girl in an elevator at the school.

He was questioned by the School Resource Officer and was asked the following:

"We are in the process of talking to the security guard that was on duty. Would there be any reason, when he switched on the microphone, that he would have heard you say, "Who's going to take their clothes off first, you or me?" I'm not saying you that you forced yourself on her or anything, but do you think she would have heard you make that statement?"

His answer was:

"*I don't recall* saying *anything* like that to her. *Maybe* I said *some things* but let's see....*no, I don't think* I told her that."

His answer consists of twenty-five words and, by my count, there are nine equivocations and negations in his answer. That's an equivocation or negation for every 2.7 words!

The equivocations are "anything," "like," "maybe," "some." and "things."

The negations are "I don't recall," "no," and "I don't think."

Are these equivocations and negations appropriate?

No, because if you are accused of making a sexual advance, especially to a student at a school where you teach and you didn't do it, you would remember what you said and didn't say. Furthermore, if you didn't say anything to the girl of a sexual nature and you are told there is a video to prove your innocence, I believe your answer would be more like, "I didn't say any such thing, she is lying. Let's see the video."

The use of a negation is also not appropriate in this context. He finally says "no" but then follows it up with "I don't think I told her that." This is not a direct denial of the accusation. It is a negation and an equivocation which is not convincing considering the circumstances.

He also states, "I don't recall, maybe I said some things." Not very convincing. When he utters the words, "Maybe I said some things," a great big red flag goes up and I am going to ask a lot of follow-up questions.

The following is a statement from a father in a shaken baby death case.

"I *cannot recall* doing *anything* out if the ordinary that day. I *do not remember* having any particular reason relating to the children. I also *do not remember* having any visitors come to my house. It was *not uncommon* for either Kathie's older sister Bonnie to walk over from her house. I *cannot remember* if either of the children were awake or asleep. *To the best of my memory* I went to work at my usual time."

First, given the context of the situation, is the equivocation and negation appropriate? No.

The baby's father can't remember anything from that morning, which is rather convenient, isn't it? He doesn't say if he saw the kids or not. He can't remember if he went to work at his normal time or not. He does attempt to place his sister-in-law, Bonnie, at the scene. Is he trying to create a false lead by implying Bonnie may know something or worse, she may have had something to do with the child's death?

Also, note that he doesn't use any contractions. His wording is rather formal, which is unusual. Most people use contractions when talking and writing. Especially in writing because they're easier and shorter to write. Not this guy.

I would deem this statement highly deceptive.

I mentioned earlier the uses of double negatives, such as "We did not find no bias in regard to the October events." This is a direct quote from Department of Justice Inspector General Michael Horowitz's report regarding FBI Deputy Assistant Director Peter Strzok's political bias and if it affected how the Crossfire Hurricane Investigation was handled. Many in the media latched on to IG Hortwitz's comment as evidence of no bias, but closer examination of his comments proves otherwise.

There are two negations in the above sentence, but they cancel each other out. If we take away the two negations, the sentence would read like this,

"We did find bias in regard to the October events."

It is much clearer, and it states unequivocally that bias did exist.

Jerry Sandusky Interview

In November 2011, Jerry Sandusky, assistant football coach at Penn State, was interview by Bob Costas concerning allegation that Sandusky had sexually assaulted multiple boys while coaching at Penn State. Here is part of the interview transcript.

Costas: Mr. Sandusky, there's a 40-count indictment. The Grand Jury report contains specific detail. There are multiple accusers, multiple eyewitnesses to various aspects of the abuse. A reasonable person says where there's this much smoke, there must be plenty of fire. What do you say?

Sandusky: I say that I'm innocent of those charges.

Costas: Innocent, completely innocent and falsely accused in every aspect?

Sandusky: Well, I could say that, you know, I have done *some* of those *things*. I have horsed around with kids. I have showered after workouts. I have hugged them, and I have touched their leg, *without intent* of sexual contact. But, um, uh, so, if you look at it that way, uh, there are *things*, that, there are *things* that *wouldn't*, you know, would be accurate.

Costas: Are you denying that you had any inappropriate sexual contact, with any of these underage boys?

Sandusky: Yes, I am.

Costas: Never touched their genitals, never engaged in oral sex.

Sandusky: Right.

Costas: What about Mike McQueary, the grad assistant, who in 2002, walked into the shower, where he says, in specific detail, that you were forcibly raping a boy who appeared to be 10 or 11 years old. That his hands were up against the shower wall and he heard rhythmic slap, slap, slapping sounds, and he described that as a rape.

Sandusky: I would say that that's false.

Costas: What would be his motive to lie?

Sandusky: You'd have to ask him that.

Costas: What did happen in the shower, the night that Mike McQueary happened upon you and the young boy?

Sandusky: Ok, we were showering and horsing *around,* and he actually turned all the showers on and was, uh, actually sliding across the, the floor, and um, and we were, as I recall, *possibly like* snapping the towel, horseplay.

Costas: In 1998 a mother confronts you about taking a shower with her son and inappropriately touching him. Two detectives eavesdrop on her conversations with you and you admit that maybe your private parts touched her son. What happened there?

Sandusky: Well, I *can't exactly recall* what was said there. Uh, in terms of, um, what I did say, was that… if he felt that way, then I was wrong…

Costas: During one of those conversations, you said, I understand I was wrong. I wish I could get forgiveness, speaking now with the mother, I know I won't get it from you. I wish I were dead. A guy falsely accused or a guy whose actions have been misinterpreted doesn't respond that way, does he?

Sandusky: I *don't know*. I *didn't say, to my recollection*, that I wished that I were dead. I was hopeful that we could reconcile things.

Costas: Shortly after that, in 2000, a janitor said that he saw you performing oral sex on a young boy in the showers in the Penn State locker facilities. Did that happen?

Sandusky: *No.*

Costas: How could somebody think they saw something as extreme and shocking as that, when it hadn't occurred, and what would possibly be their motivation to fabricate it.

Sandusky: You'd have to ask them.

Costas: It seems that if all of these accusations are false, you are the unluckiest and most persecuted man that any of us has ever heard about.

Sandusky: Heh, oh. *I don't know* what you want me to say. *I don't think* that these have been the best days of my life.

Let's analyze this statement.

Are the equivocations and negations appropriate? Some are, but most aren't.

The first equivocations and negations occur after Costas asked Sandusky if he was "innocent, completely innocent, and falsely accused in every aspect?" Sandusky responds with: "Well, I could say that, you know, I have done some of those things. I have horsed around with kids. I have showered after workouts. I have hugged them, and I have touched their legs, without intent of sexual contact. But, um, uh, so, if you look at it that way, uh, there are things, that, there are things that wouldn't, you know, would be accurate."

What are "some things?"

He then says, "there are things, there are things that wouldn't, you know, would be accurate." Huh? There are "things," what things are you talking about, Jerry? He also changes from "wouldn't" to "would" in some nonsensical verbal garbage.

Next comes this, when asked about being seen by another assistant coach sexually assaulting a young boy in the shower:

"Ok, we were showering and horsing around and he actually turned all the showers on and was, uh, actually sliding across the, the floor, and um, and we were, as I recall, possibly like snapping the towel, horseplay"

I'm pretty sure a normal person i.e. the assistant coach, would recognize a rape in progress of a young boy in the showers at Penn State. Instead Sandusky chooses to "recall possibly like snapping towels," as if these two acts are so similar that they could easily be mistaken by some casual observer.

You get the picture.

Sandusky does say one thing using equivocations that was very much true. When Costas stated the following: "It seems that if all of these accusations are false, you are the unluckiest and most persecuted man that any of us has ever heard about." Sandusky's response was: "Heh, oh. *I don't know* what you want me to say. *I don't think* that these have been the best days of my life." Ain't that the truth!

Let's look at one more statement.

This is a statement given by the live-in boyfriend of a woman whose daughter claims to have been sexually assaulted by him.

My wife had gone to the police because evidently *some things* had been said by Joann that *tended* to involve me as suspected of molesting her or *something*. I talked to the social service worker and the police detective. I told them I had *no idea* of these *things* or why these *things* were said by Joann. Pam and Joann have lived with me since last year, and we get along real good together. The only thing that I can think of is that I try to be a real father to Joann and that means that *sometimes* punishment is given to her. She *doesn't* like this, and I guess that's only natural. But as far as molesting her, I can state here and now that I have *no recollection of anything* of that nature ever occurring between us.

Are these equivocations appropriate? Hardly. He obviously wants to distance himself from these allegations.

He laughably claims to have no recollection of anything regarding the sexual assault. Ask yourself, if you did not sexually assault your girlfriend's daughter, would you say "I have no recollection of anything of that nature," or would you say, "Hell no! I didn't sexually assault her." I know which I would say. Remember, the truth is short but lies are long.

He also says that he "sometimes" punishes Joann, but says it passively, that "punishment is given to her." Once again, he is distancing himself from the action by using the passive voice. A more direct and less deceptive way of saying it would be, "I sometimes punish Joann." That statement, in the active voice, takes ownership of his actions. But I don't think this guy want to take ownership of any of his actions concerning Joann.

One last bit of advice concerning equivocation and negation. If someone says or writes, "That's about it," probe further. The phrase "That's about it" is the same as saying, "I'm done talking about this and don't ask me anymore." Which, of course, means I am going to ask a whole lot more about it.

Quick Tips

1. The use of words of equivocation and negation are strong indicators of deception. The writer/speaker is lying by omission.

2. Examples of equivocation: maybe, probably, sometimes, I think, I believe, kind of, sort of.

3. Examples of negation: no, not, never, don't recall, can't remember, I don't know, I'm not sure.

4. There is a difference between lack of memory and lack of knowledge. Lack of knowledge is a stronger indicator of truthfulness than lack of memory.

5. Always ask yourself: *Is this equivocation/negation appropriate given the context of the statement?*

CHAPTER 8:

Exploring Time

As I stated earlier, people lie either by commission or omission, omission being the easier of the two. Once again, omission is when the writer or speaker purposely omits certain facts or facets of their story to deceive the reader/listener.

When analyzing a written statement, one should always pay attention to any references to time.

When I say time, I mean reference to a specific time in the day such as ten in the morning, 2:00pm, or three o'clock.

I always annotate all of the times on a written statement in the right-hand margin of the statement. I write the reference to time exactly as the writer does. I do this so I can have a quick visual picture to see if there are any changes in the reference to time in the statement. If there is a change in a reference to time, this may be an indicator that something has changed at that point in the statement. Possibly the writer is remembering an incident that they would prefer not to disclose and, due to the stress of that memory, they change how they depict time in the statement.

For example, if the writer uses a.m. or p.m. to reference time and then drops the a.m. and p.m., that's going to catch my attention and make me ask myself, *Why the change?*

We also want to see the pace of the statement when referencing time. This is important when looking at an alibi statement. An alibi statement is a statement that accounts for your time and activities during a very specific period of time, thus providing an alibi for oneself.

When I ask for an alibi statement, I always write at the top of the page, "Tell me everything you did from when you woke up until you went to sleep." I want the writer to account for the entire day from when they woke up to when they went to sleep. Notice, I don't say, "Tell me everything you did from when you woke up to when you went to bed." Someone could go to bed and then get back up. I want all of their activities until they are asleep. Asking the question in this manner forces them to account for their activities throughout their day, which can provide insight.

It should be noted that an alibi statement will not have an incident box. So, determining if a statement is balanced and calculating the statement's PIE is virtually impossible. But by looking at the pace of the statement using the writer's time references, you can get a good idea if there are parts of the statement that they want to gloss over and other parts of the statement that they want to use to lock down their whereabouts and activities, thus providing them with a rock-solid alibi.

Change of Pace

If the writer of a statement indicates a time on every line of the statement then doesn't reference a time for eight lines in the statement, that would be considered a change of pace. This would also indicate that there is missing time in the statement. Missing time means a time when there is not a specific accounting for their activities due to the vagueness of the time references in the statement.

Once again, let's look at a statement so you can see what I'm talking about. I call this statement The Charmed Princess, because when you read the statement, it appears that she lives the life of a charmed princess.

Tell me what you did from the time you woke up until you went to sleep'

I got up this morning about **8 am,** got dressed, ate breakfast, and went shopping for 2 hours. I came home, fixed lunch, and straightened up the house. My neighbor, Martha came over and we and talked while watching the last half of the tennis match. At around **3 pm** I took the dog to the vet for a shot and stop by the garden store on the way home. I got home about **4:30 pm**, changed clothes and went to the fitness club. I did 20 minutes on the stair climber and then did my 20 minutes weight routine that consists of 3 sets of bench presses and 3 sets of curls. I plan to use the rowing machine but after waiting about 5 minutes for one to be available, I rode the bike for 15 minutes instead. I cool down for about 10 minutes, took a shower, got dressed and went home. I arrived around **6:30** fixed dinner, watched TV for a couple hours and went to bed by **10:30 pm**.

This is an alibi statement given by a woman whose husband was supposed to be murdered. She was asked by the investigators to account for her time throughout the day.

So, let's look at the pace of the statement and if there are any time changes within the statement.

The first reference to time is in the first line of the statement when she states that she got up at "8 am". Notice that she is not complying with the request to tell everything she did from the time she woke up.

The next reference to time is in line five when she states that "at around 3 pm" she took her dog to the vet. So, the wife of the victim accounts for eight hours of her day in five lines.

The next reference to time is in line six, when she arrived home at "about 4:30 pm" She accounts for one and a half hours of her day in one line. She then uses the next seven lines of her statement to account for two hours of her day detailing what she did at the gym.

Her next reference to time is in line thirteen when she arrives home "around 6:30" which is a change from how she references time in the rest of the statement. Why did she drop the "pm"?

Her last reference to time is in the last line of the statement, line fourteen, when she "went to bed at 10:30 pm". She accounts for four hours of her day in one line.

Once again, she does not comply with the request to tell everything she did that day until she went to sleep. Instead, she finishes the statement with the time when she went to bed. That may seem like nitpicking, but who is to say she went to bed and didn't get up later and perform some other activities.

So, the pace of the statement timelines is as follows:

3 lines = 8 hours

2 line = 1 ½ hours

4 lines = 2 hours

1 line = 4 hours

One can easily see that she slows the pace of her alibi statement way down later in the day. She provides an unusual amount of detail concerning her visit to the gym, but glosses over the first eight hours of her day with virtually no details of her activities. She got up, ate breakfast, went shopping, made lunch, straightened up the house, and watched a tennis match with a neighbor. Very broad and few details.

Why is she so concerned about covering herself during the hours between four and six-thirty p.m.? She provides a very specific and detailed account of her activities at the gym. When you read this part of her statement, she wants you to know she was at the gym and she has witnesses to prove it.

Now let's look at how she references time.

In all of her references to time, she consistently uses a.m. or p.m. until line ten. There she drops the a.m. and p.m. but picks it back up later in the same line. Why?

When you write the times on the right-hand margin of the statement, the inconsistency jumps out at you.

8 am

3 pm

4:30 pm

6:30

10:30 pm

And now, as Paul Harvey (Google it if you're under forty) used to say, the rest of the story.

The Charmed Princess was married to a successful businessman, but she was having an affair with a younger man. The Charmed Princess decided she liked her husband's money more that she liked him. So, with that in mind, she asked her boyfriend to kill her husband. Of course, the boyfriend knew this was a bad idea and contacted the police and told them about the scheme. The police set up a sting operation and had the boyfriend tell the Charmed Princess that he would do the dirty deed between four-thirty and six-thirty p.m. The boyfriend then called the Charmed Princess and informs her that he had taken care of her husband at 6:30 pm.

With this information, when you look at the statement again it becomes obvious what she is doing: to wit, she was creating her alibi for the time between four-thirty and six-thirty p.m.

The boyfriend agreed to make recordings of her asking him to commit the murder. During the recorded conversation, the boyfriend advised her that he would do the hit between four-thirty and six-thirty p.m. and would call her to let her know when deed was done. He called her at six-thirty, so the change in time is probably due to the stress of knowing this is the time when she was informed that her husband had been killed and that she was now complicit in his murder. She was later convicted of attempting to hire her boyfriend to kill her husband.

That's why we pay attention to these subtle changes in references of time.

Now let's look at a statement where time reference changes play a significant role.

The following is an original copy of an alibi statement written by Ralph Lynch in connection with the search for a missing six-year-old girl, Mary Jennifer Love.

(Note: this statement is written, as are all the statements in this book, verbatim with all misspellings and grammatical errors made by the authors of the statements.)

800AM GOT UP
9AM DENNEY
10 20AM OFFICE MAX
1100AM SUPER AMERIA
1115AM MID WEST WLESTLING
1204PM BIGGS
        DOWNTOWN JUSTICE CENTER
3PM MY SISTER HOUSE
330PM MY APARTMENT
      I WASHING
5PM RUNING ~~xxxxxxxxxx~~
510 DIVEING AROUND
~~xxxxxxxxxxxxxxxxx~~ 530 WASH VAN
640 STOP AT RUMPKE
730 APARTMENT
8PM OUTSIDE OF APARTMENT
    LOOKING FOR MARY

        POLICE TOLD US TO GO TO APARTMENT
1200AM WENT IN APARTMENTS
       FELL A SLEEP ON
7AM GOT UP AT SHOWER

    745 MCDONALS
           2 COFFICE
           3 EGGS SANDWICH
           1 ORANGE JICE
    OIKC
        37 WEST 7 STREET
        3 FLOOR JERRY FUQUA
    825AM PARK VAN PARKING LOT
    830AM IN OFFICE

This alibi statement is written like a time log. The writer, Ralph Lynch, worked at a solid waste-disposal facility known as Rumpke. Part of his duties at Rumpke was to maintain a work log.

In his statement, Lynch is consistent in his use of a.m. and p.m. until five p.m., with the exception of his entry, "I Washing." After that, the next four entries do not contain a.m. or p.m. They are: 5:10, 5:30, 6:40, and 7:30. The next entry is 8 p.m., when he is assisting in the search for Mary.

Why the change? Was there something going on during these times to cause him to change how he noted time?

Also, you'll notice an entry after the 5:10 entry that has been written then scribbled out. This is exactly how Lynch wrote his statement. He wrote "730 p.m. Apartment", then decided to change it to "530 Wash van." It appears that Lynch wanted to provide more details for his alibi for the time between 5:10 p.m. and 8:00 p.m. He also wanted to reveal the fact that he washed his van, just in case someone saw him doing that.

Also, worth noting is his entry at "5 PM Runing," and then the next entry "510 Diveing around." The timeline doesn't make sense. Who runs for ten minutes and then is driving around? (Runing and diveing are misspelled words for running and driving.)

This statement contains several red flags. What does "washing" mean? "Runing" for ten minutes and the "diveing around"? Why the obliterated 7:30 p.m. entry?

Here's the back story of what happened.

On June 24, 1998, Lynch lured six-year-old Mary Jennifer Love into his apartment in Coletrain Township, Hamilton County, Ohio. Lynch began to molest the little girl and, to stifle her screams, he strangled her.

Once she was dead, Lynch took Love to the bathtub, where he sexually abused her lifeless body. He then placed her body in a vacuum cleaner box and removed it from his apartment. He dumped her body in a wooded lot off of

Breezy Acres, a street in the area, and covered it with an old rug. He disposed of her clothing at his employer's worksite.

Love's parents alerted police that she was missing. A search of the neighborhood was unsuccessful. Local law enforcement and FBI agents canvassed the neighborhood, looking for persons who had seen Love. The agents interviewed Lynch. His demeanor aroused their interest in him. He said that he had recently met Love and spoken to her, but had no knowledge of her whereabouts.

The Hamilton County Sheriff investigators also questioned Lynch. He was cooperative and went to the police station for more questioning. At the station, another officer, not involved in the search for Love, recognized Lynch and informed investigators that he had previously arrested Lynch for exposing himself to a child.

During this interview, Lynch admitted touching young girls in his apartment in the past. He also admitted that he had touched Love, but outside his apartment. Lynch was permitted to leave the station when the interview concluded.

On July 3, 1998, at the request of the police, Lynch returned to the station. After he executed another waiver of rights form, police questioned Lynch about inconsistencies in his previous statements. During five hours of questioning, he admitted harboring sexual fantasies about children and finally confessed, "She's on Breezy Acres." He then led the police to Love's remains and admitted that he was responsible for her death.

In his confession, Lynch admitted inviting Love into his apartment to eat popcorn and watch television, engaging in sexual contact with her, and, when she screamed, placing his hands around her neck and strangling her for three minutes. Lynch alleged that his intent was to stop the screaming, not to kill her.

Lynch was charged with aggravated murder with the death-penalty specifications, based on aggregating circumstances that the crime was committed during the commission of other felonies (rape and kidnapping), and that the victim was a child under thirteen years of age. He was found guilty and sentenced to death in October 1999.

Go back and re-read the statement. With Lynch's confession, the following entries become much more significant:

330 PM My apartment

The next entry is Washing. This is probably when he placed Love's body in the bathtub to sexually assault her post death, and then to wash the body to eliminate any trace evidence such as semen. Because of the situation Lynch was in at this point, it is not surprising that he changed his time annotation.

510 Diveing (sic) around is probably alluding to Lynch driving around with Love's body looking for a dumpsite.

530 Wash Van most likely means he washed his van to destroy forensic trace evidence such as hair and fibers.

640 Stop at Rumpke. This is when and where Lynch dumped Love's clothing.

730 Apartment. He returns to the scene of the crime.

The first time I became aware of the importance of time in a person's statement occurred in my first child-abduction case.

On February 26, 1997, a seven-year girl named Samantha Zaldivar was reported missing by her mother, Rachel Stra, to the Wyoming County Sheriff's Office, Wyoming County, New York. According to Stra, Zaldivar had left to catch the school bus at approximately 7:30 a.m. on February 26, but never returned home after school. After contacting the school, Stra was informed that Zaldivar never attended school on February 26.

By February 27, the Buffalo FBI Field Office was notified and immediately dispatched agents to assist in the investigation. I was assigned to the Violent Crimes Squad, which investigates child abductions and was deployed by my supervisor, Jack McDonnell, to go to Wyoming County to provided whatever assistance was needed. Within a day, the FBI had opened a child-abduction investigation and I was assigned as the co-case agent with Special Agent Tom Doktor.

Zaldivar lived with her mother, Stra, her mother's live-in boyfriend, Angel Colon, and her two younger half-sisters.

Colon was a Miami, Florida, native with a history of drug use and petty crimes.

According to Stra and Colon, on the night of February 25, Colon spent the evening with Zaldivar while Stra was attending night school. Stra came home and fell asleep on the couch and then later moved to her bedroom and slept in the next morning while Colon got Zaldivar off to school.

As with any child-abduction investigation, the first people to look at are the parents. Each parent is interviewed separately to see if their stories are consistent with each other. These are very in-depth interviews, giving the parents a chance to provide an alibi.

By this time in the investigation, the FBI Evidence Response Team led by Special Agent Tim Crino, had collected enough forensic evidence from Zaldivar's bedroom to led us to believe that she may have been sexually assaulted and the assault may have ended in murder. We needed to interview Colon to find out what happened the night before the disappearance.

SA Tom Doktor and I conducted the interview of Colon. We asked Colon to account for his time for the evening of February 25 when he was alone with Zaldivar. Colon was experienced in dealing with law enforcement due to his many run-ins with the law in Florida. He was not someone who would normally help law enforcement.

Colon recounted his activities for the day and night of February 25. He was specific with times for his activities throughout the day and evening until the time Zaldivar went to bed. He told us the time he picked Zaldivar's half-sisters up from day care, when they got home, when Zaldivar arrived home from school, when he made the kids dinner, and when he gave them a bath. According to Colon, Zaldivar went to bed at 9:00 p.m.

After 9:00 p.m., Colon gave no more specific times for his activities for the rest of the evening and night. He didn't remember when Stra came home from night school and couldn't remember when they went to bed or what he watched on TV. The next timeline he gave was that he got Zaldivar up on the morning of February 26 and she left to catch the school bus at approximately 7:30 a.m.

I remember thinking at the time that there was a big hole in his timeline and alibi. After that interview, I was further convinced that Colon was involved in Zaldivar's disappearance.

We conducted a thorough investigation and continued to build a possible murder case against Colon, but without a body, we were stuck.

In May 1997, a farmer was plowing a field approximately a half mile from Zaldivar's home, preparing it for spring planting. While riding on his tractor, he saw something purple sticking up out of the ground. When he got off his tractor to see what it was, he realized it was a child's arm and the purple was the child's coat.

He called the Wyoming Sheriff's Office. I, SA Doktor, and SA Crino along with his Evidence Response Team went to the field and over the next twelve hours recovered Zaldivar's body from where she had been buried. Due to the cold temperature of the ground from February to May, there was almost no decomposition of Zaldivar's body.

With the evidence obtained during the investigation along with the forensic evidence obtained from the victim's body, the Wyoming County District Attorney charged Colon with first-degree capital murder. Colon eventually pled to second-degree murder and is still serving a twenty-five years to life sentence in Attica.

The point of this story is this: I knew that there was something wrong with Colon's explanations, but I didn't really know why I knew it. If I had known what I am teaching you, the reader of this book, I would have been able to conduct a much better interview of not only Colon but many other people in this case.

So, in summary, always note any references to time in a statement. As you can see, they can provide a plethora of leads to pursue and questions to ask.

Quick Tips

1. Look for missing time since most people lie by omission.

   8:10 a.m.

   9:03 a.m.

   10:15 a.m.

   GAP

   1:45 p.m.

   3:20 p.m.

2. Look for changes in pace in the timeline.

   One line per hour

   one line per hour

   Thirteen lines per hour (ALIBI)

   One line per hour

   One line per hour

3. Look for changes in how time is referenced.

   10 AM

   2:00 p.m.

   2pm

   7:00

Very specific about time and then a change to a vague reference to time

versus

Very vague about time and then a change to a specific reference to time

SECTION 2:

Language Used to Deceive

CHAPTER 9:

Cast of Characters and Nouns

Statements are like movies. They all have a cast of characters. These are the people who are introduced into the statement by the writer or speaker. Why is that important, you ask? Let's do a quick exercise and then I'll tell you why.

On a piece of paper, write three lists:

1. All of the members of your immediate family, including your pets if you so choose

2. Three months of the year

3. Three states

Now set these lists to the side and we'll get back to them soon.

Seth Stephen Davidowitz is the author of the book, *Everybody Lies: Big Data, New Data, and What the Internet Can Tell Us About Who We Really Are. .* He is a self-proclaimed "internet data expert" (Beware of experts!) who tracks "the digital trails that people leave as they make their way across the web." Davidowitz uses a tool known as Google Trends to track how frequently a word or phrase is used for Google searches on the Internet.

During the course of his research, Davidowitz looked at the results of Google searches of the two main candidates during the 2016 presidential election, Donald Trump and Hillary Clinton. Davidowitz was surprised to learn that whoever's name was placed in the search bar first turned out to be a good barometer of that candidate's popularity in that particular region or state. Davidowitz writes: "During the 2016 election between Trump and Clinton, some people search for "Trump Clinton polls". Others look for highlights from the "Clinton Trump debate". In fact, 12% of search queries with Trump also includes the word Clinton. More than one quarter of search queries with Clinton also include the word Trump. We have found that these seemingly neutral searches may actually give us some clues as to which candidate a person supports. How? The order in which the candidates appear. Our research suggests that a person is significantly more likely to put the candidate they support first in a search that includes both candidate's names.

In the previous three elections, the candidate who appeared first and in more searches received the most votes. More interesting, the order the candidates were searched was predictive of which way a particular state would go.

The order in which candidates are searched also seem to contain information that polls can miss. In the 2012 election between Obama and Republican Mitt Romney, Nate Silver, the virtuoso statistician and journalist, accurately predicted the results of all 50 states. However, we found that the states that listed Romney before Obama in searches most frequently, Romney actually did better than Silver have predicted. In states that most frequently listed Obama before Romney, Obama did better than Silver had predicted."

Davidowitz may have been surprised with these results, but I'm not.

Human nature is such that we list what we favor first over someone or something we don't. When the two candidates are listed together, the searcher must choose who they want to list first. We just default to our preferred candidate. In this case, your cast of characters are Trump/Clinton or Clinton/Trump.

Now let's look at your lists.

The chances are the list of your immediate family members will show that you listed either yourself or your wife first and then your children and possibly pets. If you listed your wife first and then yourself, why did you do that? How did you choose to list your children if you have more than one? Did you go by age, by gender, by sex, or by how well you like them? If you listed your pets, which one got top billing?

What three months did you pick and why did you pick them? Many will list their birth month as their first month. Some will list their spouse's birth month or maybe their anniversary. The point is, why did you pick this particular month?

For the three states, chances are you chose the current state where you reside. The second state could be the state where you were born or the state where you met your spouse. Again, why that state?

The point is that people have preferences just like they have biases. Experience has shown that people always have a reason, either consciously or unconsciously, for how they rank people and objects in their lives.

I know for myself that whenever I sign a birthday, anniversary, or thank you card, I always sign it in the following order: Frank, Karrie (my wife), Natali (my daughter), and our two beagles, Hunter and Honey. I always list Hunter first because he's my dog and he's my favorite. If my wife signs a card, she will always list me first, (because she knows which side her bread is buttered on!) herself, Natali, then Honey, and finally Hunter. When I asked her why she listed Honey before Hunter, she explained that Honey is her dog.

So how do we use this information?

Well, when I interview someone, I always ask them to tell me who is in their immediate family. I write down the order that they list the family members and if they make any proper introductions of their family.

For instance, if the person I am interviewing lists his wife but does not identify her as his wife, just uses her name, I will note that. That lack of proper introduction may indicate that there is some distance or strain in the relationship.

I also want to know who has the most influence in that person's life. This
information can be used during the interview or interrogation as leverage to
move the interviewee from uncooperative to cooperative.

This information can also be used when coaching or counseling someone.
For instance, say you are a financial coach working with a couple about budget-
ing and paying off debt and the husband is being reluctant about creating the
budget. Knowing who is the most important person to him would be useful,
which in this case is his wife, Janice. In this case, I would say something along
the lines of, "I know how important this is to you and Janice to get your finances
under control. You want to take care of Janice and the kids, and the best way
to do that is to be financially sound. Just think about how happy and proud
Janice would be if you could achieve that goal. You're a good man and a strong,
proud man. Janice needs you to be strong for her and help her achieve this goal."
I would say this while Janice looks lovingly at him. How could he resist? He
might, but I've made it much harder to do because I know who is important to
him and used that knowledge to move him from uncooperative to cooperative.

When analyzing a statement, I always write down in the left-hand margin
of the statement the name or identity of the person the first time they appear in
the statement. In this manner I can create the cast of characters that the writer
or speaker uses in the statement, which gives me insight into who may be the
most important or influential person to the writer or speaker.

Let's revisit the Susan Smith statement from chapter 3. Who is in her cast
of characters?

1 I arrived home around 6:00 p.m. on
2 Tuesday, October 25, 1994. It had been
3 an upsetting day for me. When I
4 walked in the door, my phone was ringing
5 but before I could answer it, they
6 hung up. I have call return on my
7 phone so I dialed back and it was
8 my mom. I asked her if she was
9 going to be home because I might
10 come over. (When I am upset, I have
11 to go somewhere or do something). She
12 told me what she was going to Nick's
13 ball game at 7:00 and it would
14 probably only last an hour so she
15 would be back home sometime after
16 8:00. She asked me if she wanted me
17 to just let her come by my house
18 and I told her no what I would
19 rather come see her. (She didn't know
20 what I was upset). We ended the
21 conversation with me planning on coming
22 to her house. I hung up the phone
23 and went into the living room w/ Michael
24 ? Alex. If I recall correctly, he put a
25 movie in the VCR. I went into the
26 kitchen and ~~was~~ tried to find them

27 Something to eat. I decided to fix
28 them a pizza. They played in
29 the meantime and I played with
30 them. Because of my conversation with
31 Tom earlier, I was concerned about
32 him and I knew that he was at
33 Hickory Nuts with Susan Brown. So I
34 called Hickory Nuts to talk to Susan
35 to see how Tom was. I could
36 tell by talking to her that she couldn't
37 say much about Tom because Tom was
38 sitting beside her. She told me she
39 would call me later and talk to me.
40 I said O.K. I really don't remember
41 what else I did after that. Before I
42 left that night I also received a call
43 from David. He said he was just
44 calling to see what we were doing and
45 to just chit chat. He could tell that
46 something was bothering me and he
47 asked me what was wrong. I told
48 him that I couldn't tell him. He
49 said you can tell me anything and I
50 said not this. We ended the conversation
51 with him saying that if I needed him
52 to call him. After that phone call, I

53 began to prepare a diaper bag
54 for Michael & Alex. Since I was
55 going to my mom's I was just going
56 to go ahead and give them a bath
57 at her house so I got them some
58 pajamas ready and I fixed Alex a
59 bottle. It was around 8:00 or a little
60 after when I left the house. When I
61 left you could tell that I had been
62 crying, so I said we will just ride
63 around a little while because I
64 didn't want my mom know that I
65 had been upset so we rode around
66 all over Union and up to Jonesville
67 and I was riding I just thought
68 that Michael & Alex hadn't seen
69 Mitch in a while so I asked Michael
70 if he wanted to go see Mitch and he
71 told me yes. So I said to myself
72 we will go see Mitch and I'll call
73 my mom from there and let her know
74 that I wasn't coming over there.
75 Unfortunately I never made it to
76 Mitch's. I had stopped at the red
77 light at Monarch Mill and while I
78 was waiting for the light to change

79 a black man jumped in my car, put
80 a gun to my side and said "Drive or
81 I'll kill you." I went into hysterics
82 and started screaming Why are you
83 doing this? What do you want? He just
84 told me to shut up and drive or
85 he would kill me. Michael asked me
86 who that man was and what was
87 wrong. I tried to comfort him and
88 tell him that everything would be
89 O.K. The black man allowed me to
90 talk to Michael and Alex a couple
91 of times but when he told me that
92 was enough. I continued to drive and
93 was praying to the Lord to take
94 care of me and my children. Out of
95 nowhere, the black man told me to
96 stop. It was odd to me that he
97 was asking me to stop right
98 there in the middle of the road on
99 that highway. I questioned him about
100 stopping and he told me right quick
101 again to stop the car right now. I
102 was going to
103 pull over on the side of the road and
104 stop but he told me no, to stop right

105 here. He then told me to get out
106 of the car or I'm going to kill you and I opened my car
107 door and told him what I have to
108 get my babies and as he was moving
109 over to the driver's seat he was
110 pushing me out of the car and he
111 told me that he didn't have time and
112 I screamed and begged for him to
113 please let me get my children and
114 he said again that he didn't have
115 time but told me that he would
116 not hurt my children. He shut the
117 door and took off. I dropped to the
118 road like a ton of bricks, screaming
119 for someone to please help me! I
120 went totally numb. I then jumped up
121 and started running up the road
122 continuing to scream for help. I ran to
123 the closest house that had lights on.
124 I could barely see because it was so
125 dark. I got on this front porch and
126 I banged on the door continuing to cry
127 for help. A lady and man opened the
128 door and saw that I was in trouble
129 but I could hardly tell her what was
130 wrong. She took me into her house

and tryed to calm me enough so I could
tell her what had happened. Once
they knew what had happened, they
immediately phoned the police. As I
sat in that lady's house, I prayed and
prayed that my children be o.k. I
was devastated, I was hysterical, I
couldn't understand why!!

Her cast of characters is:

- "My mom"
- "Nick" (her brother)
- "Michael and Alex" (her children)
- "Tom" (Findlay) (her estranged boyfriend)
- "Susan Brown" (who Tom Findlay was seeing that night)
- "David" (Smith) (her estranged husband)
- "Mitch" (a friend)
- "A black man" (the fictional carjacker/kidnapper)

When I look at the above cast, a couple of things jump out at me.

First, Smith lists Tom Findlay long before her husband. Why did she do that? She was estranged from David Smith, but actively pursuing a relationship with Findlay. With that in mind, it makes sense that she would list Findlay before her husband. Findlay is her preference, over David Smith.

Second, she mentions Susan Brown, her direct competition for Tom Findlay's affections, which make her significant to Smith.

Finally, the most influential person in the whole story, "a black man," the alleged kidnapper, was listed last. Why is the main character of the story listed last?

As I explained earlier, her statement is completely unbalanced. Smith also includes so much extraneous information that the introduction of the fictional carjacker/kidnapper comes very late in the story. If this was an actual incident, Smith would have most likely introduced the carjacker/kidnapper much earlier in the story and he would have a much higher billing in the cast of characters.

Changes in Nouns

Sometimes, the way people are referred to in statements changes over the course of the statement. These changes generally reflect a change in the person's status to the writer/speaker.

There is a statement I use in my training seminars, written by a homicide suspect, which is an excellent example of how characters can change and provides insight into how the writer thinks of this person.

The main homicide suspect is asked to provide a statement concerning who he thought had committed the murder. In the statement, the suspect initially uses the term murderer, then later changes it to the killer, which then changes to the maniac, and finally to the poor, sick man.

Each change softened the character and makes him progressively more sympathetic. By referring to him as the maniac and the poor, sick man, the writer is transmitting that the murderer is not responsible for his actions due to his mental condition. Not surprisingly, the statement writer eventually confessed to the murder.

Now let's take a look at a fun little statement from Ocean City, Maryland. I call this statement Lime Green Shirt Dude. (Italics added)

9/3/05 2:00 am there I was… feelin sexy like usual. **Ben** + I left Fish tails + we were doin what two half-light guys would do. Lookin for someone to play with like a woman type. We got on bus + bulshited with people + these **two guys** told us they had a party to go to with only women. That was good. We had stopped at a couple of peoples places completely randomly, but they invited us. So after stopping at a couple of places we followed **these dudes** to the apperant party + we walked up an ocean front side street. I was chillen with **lime green shirt dude** + he made a weird advance, I would call it sexual to destract me. + it did just that. When I finally became uncomfortable I realized that something weird was in the air. I have a sence for that thing so seriously when I turn around ***my cousin*** was straight up knocted the fxxked out in a bush. I saw the ***guy in a white polo*** which we had been walken with for a couple of blockes, tearin ass towards the beach. Me not really being so swift had no clue that ***Ben*** just got robbed until I asked him. Then I felt kinda stupid because I never saw it coming. I ran around the beach to catch him but had no Idea were he went. My Statement is 100% true + come from the heart.

OCEAN CITY POLICE DEPARTMENT
WITNESS   Ocean City, Maryland   DATE _____
                                                                   CC# _____

Name X ████████████████████

Address X ████████████████████

Date of Birth ████████████   Phone X ████████████

Seasonal Address _____

Seasonal Phone _____

X 9/3/05 2:00 am there I was... fellin sexy
like usual. Ben + I left Fish tails + We
were doin what two half lidt guys world
do. Lookin for someone to play with like a woman
type. We got on bus + bullshitted with
people + these two guys told us they
had a party to go to with only women.
That was good. We had stopped at
a couple of peoples places completely
romdomly, but they invited us. So after
Stoppin at a couple of places we followed
these dudes to the apparent party. + we
walked up an ocean front side street. I was
chillen with lime green shirt dude + he made a
weird advance. I would call it sexual to destrict
me. + It did just that. When I finally became
uncomfortable I realized that something wierd was in

Signature X ████████████████

OFC Signature ████████

Form 102   Revised 3/1/95

OCEAN CITY POLICE DEPARTMENT
Ocean City, Maryland

CC#_____

Date_____

Statement of: _____

the air. I have a sence for that thing. So seriously when I turn around my cousin was streight up knocked the f××ked out in a bush. I saw the guy in a white polo which we had been walken with for a couple of blocks, tearin ass towards the beach. Me not really being so swift had no clue that Ben just got robbed until I asked him. Then I felt kinda stupid because I never seen I coming. I ran around the beach to catch him, but had no Idea were he went. My statement is 100% true + come from the heart.

Signature _____

OFC Signature _____

Form 102A

Revised 3/1/95

There are a lot of crazy things in this statement.

The first person introduced is Ben. The next characters introduced are "these two guys," which changes to "these dudes," then to "lime green shirt dude" and the "the guy in the white polo shirt." When the writer realizes Ben has been injured, he refers to him as "my cousin." The writer claims a familial tie to Ben when he senses danger, but changes it back to Ben after the danger has passed. You can also see the progression of the two other characters from the mundane "these two guys" to the friendlier "these dudes."

And he ends the statement asserting that his statement is "100 percent true and comes from the heart." Well, if it comes from the heart, then call me a believer!

Here is one more example of changing nouns. The following statement is from a husband who claimed his wife drowned while boating.

My wife and I left home about 9 a.m. and went to the marina where we keep our boat. *My wife* and I left the marina in the boat around 10:30 a.m. I picked up some fuel and odds and ends at the boat stored then she and I headed for Captain's Cove, about 5 miles out. Arriving around 11:30 a.m. I anchored the boat and then *my wife* and I started to swim. It was about 11:50 when I noticed that *Sandi* was nowhere to be found.

The writer uses the noun "my wife" three times, but changes to "Sandi" when he noticed she was "nowhere to be found." Why the change?

Experience has shown that perpetrators often find it difficult to admit to harming family members, so they distance themselves by dropping the familiar reference. In this case, he distanced himself from the spousal relationship by using "Sandi" instead of "my wife" after he drowned her.

Always be alert to how people, places, and objects are referred to. If a noun changes, ask yourself, *Why?*

Quick Tips

1. Every statement and story has a cast of characters.

2. Rule of thumb: The earlier a person shows up in a statement, the more important that person is. The less important a person is, the later they will arrive in the statement.

3. When people, places, and objects are listed in a statement, there is always a reason for their ranking, even if the person making the statement doesn't know it.

4. Pay attention to when nouns change. Always ask, *Why the change?*

CHAPTER 10:

Verbs: Action Heroes of Language

And now we finally come to the section of the book you've been waiting for: Verbs!

Wait, where are you going? Don't leave. I promise this isn't going to be like eighth-grade English. What I am about to tell you will be interesting and will possibly change your life! Also, if you hang in there, I will tell you about the six verbs I see most often used for deception.

Verbs are the action heroes of language. Verbs indicate action taken by someone or something. Verbs are dynamic.

But verbs can also be deceptive. They can be used to hide actions taken. They can tell us when someone is being deceptive by the tense they use. Verbs can indicate when an activity is interrupted. Verbs will tell us when someone is talking even when they don't tell us. Passive-voice verbs can indicate that the speaker is distancing themselves from an action.

Present versus Past-Tense Verbs

Let's start with verb tense. When using DLA, I am most concerned about present tense versus past tense when it comes to verbs.

To state the obvious, past tense should refer to past events, whereas present tense refers to current events. Using a present-tense verb when talking about an event in the past makes no sense. Present is present and the past is the past, right?

Unless they are fabricating a story.

You see, when we fabricate a story, we almost always use present-tense verbs. Why? Because when we are making up a story, we are doing it in the present, not the past so we automatically use present-tense verbs. We aren't recalling events, we are creating them, right now.

What is really interesting is when the speaker/writer goes from past tense to present tense and then back to past tense. This almost always indicates deception.

Let's look at an example. Consider the following statement:

"It happened Saturday night. I went out on my back deck to water the plants. It was almost dark. A man ran out of the bushes. He came onto the deck, grabbed me, and knocked me down."

This statement makes sense because all of the verbs are in past tense because the writer is speaking about a past event. But what happens if we change a few of these verbs?

"It happened Saturday night. I went out on my back deck to water the plants. It was almost dark. A man runs out of the bushes. He comes onto the deck, grabs me, and knocks me down."

The speaker goes from past tense to present tense. Why? Is she fabricating a story to explain away something we don't know about? When you read the statement, you can almost feel the incongruity. You can see where the speaker goes from the past to the present.

Now some will say, "Frank, come on. The person changes to the present tense because they are reliving the incident." Maybe, maybe not. I do know this: this inconsistency is an indicator of deception, and I would explore this change in tense closely.

Now let's look at a statement concerning an automobile accident. Pick out where the writer changes from past tense to present tense and then back to past tense.

"I was driving along on route 3 looking at the scenery. I was taking my time because I was early for my appointment. There was a woman following me kind of close but I didn't think much of it because I was not blocking traffic. She had plenty of room to pass me if she wanted to. After a couple of miles, she moved along side of me and stayed there for some time. When I glanced in her direction she looked at me like I was dirt. We drive like this for some time and then she cuts right in front of me. I don't see her coming until it's too late. We pulled off the road and she started screaming that I ran into her. "

Do you see it? Let me show you.

"I was driving along on route 3 looking at the scenery. I was taking my time because I was early for my appointment. There was a woman following me kind of close, but I didn't think much of it because I was not blocking traffic. She had plenty of room to pass me if she wanted to. After a couple of miles, she moved along side of me and stayed there for some time. When I glanced in her direction, she looked at me like I was dirt. We ***drive*** like this for some time and then she ***cuts*** right in front of me. I ***don't*** see her coming until it's too late. We pulled off the road and she started screaming that I ran into her. "

The writer uses past-tense verbs until line six, where he changes to present tense. This occurs immediately after "She looked at me like I was dirt." Suddenly, he uses present tense to tell us about the accident and how she caused the accident by pulling in front of him, "she cuts in front of me." The writer then reverts to past tense.

The writer obviously knows how to use the proper tense when discussing past events, so we should question why he changes tense. Is he reliving an event or fabricating? This is for the interviewer to determine.

Over my career, I investigated numerous child abductions. I was a member of the elite FBI Child Abduction Rapid Deployment (CARD) Team. The CARD Team is a select group of FBI agents with an expertise in child abduction investigations who are deployed to assist local law enforcement agencies and other FBI offices when a child abduction occurs.

When investigating a child abduction, one of the first things we looked at is the use of verb tense when referring to the abducted child. If the mother or father used a past-tense verb to refer to the child, it was a big red flag. There is ample evidence that shows parents will maintain hope for years that their child will be returned and use present tense when talking about the child. So, using past-tense verbs to describe an unrecovered child is unusual, especially shortly after the abduction.

Take the case of Melissa Brannen.

Melissa was a six-year-old girl living in Lorton, Virginia when, on December 3, 1989, she was abducted from a neighborhood Christmas party. Eventually, Caleb Hughes, a groundskeeper for the apartment complex where Melissa lived, was charged with Melissa's abduction. In 1991, Hughes was convicted of child abduction and sentenced to 50 years.

In 1999, a *Washington Post* interview of Melissa's mother, Tammy Brannen Graybill, showed that hope truly never fades when the body of the abducted child hasn't been found.

In the interview, it is obvious that no real closure has taken place. Graybill still hoped that Melissa would be recovered. Graybill said in the interview, "I think that there's a very slim possibility that Caleb met someone and handed her off. I still have dreams of being reunited with her, especially around this time of year and on her birthday."

Even though Graybill is married, she kept her name Brannen and is listed in the phone book as Tammy Brannen Graybill just in case Melissa ever comes looking for her.

Graybill never uses the past tense when talking about Melissa. Melissa is not gone in her mind because she has no definitive proof that she is dead. Hughes refused to provide any information about Melissa's whereabouts and her body was never recovered. Although thirty years have passed, I bet Graybill still refers to Melissa in the present tense.

Juxtapose Tammy Brannen Graybill to Susan Smith.

South Carolina Law Enforcement Division (SLED) Agent David A. Caldwell questioned Smith concerning the alleged abduction of her two sons. Agent Caldwell asked Smith the following question, "We have information that you have a boyfriend, Tom Findlay, and that he is not interested in pursuing a relationship with you because of your children. Did this fact play any role or have any bearing on the disappearance of your children?"

Smith's response was, "No man would make me hurt my children. They were my life."

She knew her children were dead when she made this statement. They were in the past for her.

I have personally seen this happen in child abduction cases.

I recall a case from Tampa, Florida, where a young mother claimed that her son had been abducted from his bedroom during the night. The mother was born in Vietnam and had been adopted as a child by a couple who lived in Buffalo, New York.

I received a lead from the Tampa Field office asking me to interview the mother's adoptive parents, extended family, and friends for further background. The parents painted a picture of a troubled young woman who had a wild side to her. She became a single parent, but never really took to being a mother.

She had moved from Buffalo to Tampa to live with her adoptive grandparents. Eventually, she moved into an apartment on her own with her infant son.

The mother reported that she left the window in her son's room open the night before and someone cut the window screen and took her son from his room. An examination of the screen showed a clean cut on one corner of the screen and no tearing, which would have been evident if an adult had reached through the window to take the child. Additionally, the cut was too small for an adult to lean through to grab the child. This raised the suspicions of the Tampa FBI agents.

The mother's adoptive parents identified several of their daughter's friends who maintained contact with her. When I interviewed the friends, they all showed sincere remorse and sympathy for their friend. One friend said she had been contact with the mother and showed me a message the mother had texted her the morning after the alleged abduction. Within the text was this statement, "He was such a good boy." My heart dropped. I knew we would not find this child alive. She had already moved on.

Approximately a week later, the mother was interviewed by Nancy Grace on CNN. The interview started out fine, but become contentious when the mother couldn't and wouldn't answer basic questions such as where she went and what she did on the day of the child's abduction. As I watched the interview, I could see Grace becoming more incredulous about the mother's story of abduction. Being a former prosecutor, Grace started asking pointed questions. The mother became angry and abruptly hung up on Grace in the middle of the nationally televised interview. Later the same day, the mother wrote a suicide note blaming law enforcement and the media for her predicament, placed a shotgun in her mouth, and committed suicide in her grandparent's bedroom. Nowhere in the note does she indicate the fate of her son. To date, the child's body has not been found.

Verbs of Communication

Many times, we use verbs to indicate communication between people and that communication can take many forms. We will say we told so and so something. We said this or that. I asked for something. Those examples are easy to recognize.

But sometimes we use words and phrases to camouflage communication.

If I tell you that my wife and I watched TV all evening, did we talk? Surely someone said something, right?

If you say that you met Jim for coffee, can we assume that you two talked? Most likely.

You got together with Margie for lunch. Did you two talk?

When someone uses activities to mask communications, always ask yourself, *What did they talk about?*

For clarification, here is a list of verbs of communication:

- Talked
- Spoke
- Chatted
- Discussed
- Argued
- Deliberated
- Disagreed
- Called

Some examples of masked verbs of communications:

- IM'ed
- Texted
- Emailed
- Got together
- Ate lunch

- Watched TV
- Drove
- Met for coffee
- Hooked up

Let's look at a statement with verbs of communication.

"I got up around 6 a.m. while he stayed in bed. I took Harley, my lab, for a walk since I knew no one around here was going to take the time to walk him. We go back, I showered, & made myself some oatmeal. He came down about 8 am & he and I *talked.* And then I left to pick up Stan, my partner from work about 8:20. Met Stan and we *drove* in his car the 5 1/2 hrs to Richmond. We *chatted* the whole way. We got to our rooms at 2 p.m. and I started to get cleaned up. That's about it."

In this statement there are three verbs of communication, two open and one masked. The open verbs of communication are talked and chatted. The masked verb of communication is drove. They drove for five and a half hours to Richmond. Do you think they talked?

A couple of other things in this statement are interesting. The first thing that jumps out is the lack of identifying who "he" is. We assume "he" is alluding to her husband or boyfriend. Regardless, not giving any relationship to "he" indicates that the relationship is strained. Unlike Harley, her lab, and Stan, her partner. She likes them!

The other thing that I noticed was the use of a verb of incomplete action, "started" in the next-to-last sentence. We will address that in the next section.

The last thing is the statement, "That's about it." Whenever someone ends a statement with, "That's about it," rest assured that there is more to tell, they just don't want to. What they are really saying is, "I told you everything. Don't ask me anything more," which, of course, makes me ask more questions.

Let's look at a statement about a store robbery. The statement is given by the clerk who was on duty the night of the robbery.

Tell me what happened.

I was standing in the back-storage room ***talking*** to Jane Smith on the phone. A black man in his late 20's to early thirties came out of the bathroom and handed me a note ***saying*** – I have a gun don't do anything stupid or I'll kill you. I got off the phone with Jane. He ***showed*** me the gun (medium pistol). He ***thought*** the money was in the candy room and ***demanded*** to go in. I took him in there and ***showed*** him around. He ***wanted to know*** where all the money was and how much there was. I ***told*** him. I also ***told*** him it would take 10 minutes to open the safe. He ***said*** to play it cool and open it while he waited. I set the timer and ***walked*** him around the store. After about 5 minutes I ***walked*** him back to the front and took the money out of both end registers. I put the safe money together with it in a blue zipper bag, then put the bag in a small box. I ***walked*** him to the back of the store. He left the box on the floor, put the bag up his shirt, then ***told*** me to walk him out.

The store clerk used the masked verb of communication "walked" several times. The use of "walked" masks the fact that the robber and the clerk are communicating throughout the robbery.

Also, the verb "showed" seems out of place. It is too casual for the situation. The statement sounds like the clerk is giving the robber a tour of the store.

Could this be a case of an inside job?

Of course! That's what it turned out to be. The clerk let his friend into the store and gave him the money to split later.

The whole tone of the statement was off because of the verbs used.

Before I move on, I want to make some distinction between the following verbs of communication.

Said is soft in nature and indicates a one-sided conversation.

Told is firmer in nature and more assertive.

Stated or **advised** is the same as said but indicate a higher degree of stress and could indicate a sensitive point in the narrative.

Ask or **asked** is softer and indicates politeness. Criminals and assailants don't ask, they tell and demand.

When analyzing verbs of communication, ask who is using the more assertive verbs of communication. It may indicate dominance in a relationship or a desire to be dominant.

Verbs of Interrupted Action

Verbs of interrupted action skip over time and move the story along.

Verbs of interrupted action indicate an action or activity started by the speaker/writer, but do not indicate completion of the action. The question that must be asked is, "Was the action completed?" and "If not, what interrupted the action?"

Some common verbs of interrupted action are:

- Began
- Started
- Commenced
- Initiated
- proceeded
- Tried
- Attempted

Here is an example of a verb of interrupted action. "I started to pack my suitcase. Then I drove to the airport."

Did the speaker/writer finish packing her suitcase? We don't know. We assume they did, but therein lies the deceptive language. They are not telling you they finished packing, they are letting you, the listener, answer the question. Can you accurately say they finished packing? No.

The simplest way to say the above statement with no deceptive language is to state the following, "I packed my suitcase and drove to the airport." Remember, the truth is almost always shorter than a lie.

Here is an excerpt from a statement given by a man charged with a double homicide. According to the man, his two cohorts, Jimmy and Snoot, pressured him into robbing an elderly woman of her prescription drugs.

Jimmy and Snoot drove the man to the woman's house, gave him a gun, and told him to wait for their call. The man sat on the steps of the woman's house and waited. Unfortunately for Jimmy and Snoot, they buttdialed our man. When his phone rang, he answered it and overheard Jimmy and Snoot laughing and discussing how they intended to cut him out of the deal and kill him. Naturally, he was pretty upset and decided to take action. He writes:

"So I put a bullet in the chamber and *started* walking back to the car an (sic) they were still laughing when I walked up. So I opened my door an (sic) *started* getting in an (sic) he said bitch you do it yet an (sic) I said yeah an (sic) *started* reaching back for the drugs an (sic) I pulled the gun an (sic) fired fast one at him an (sic) one at Snoot but Snoot was still breathing. So then he turned around and *tried* to fight an (sic) choke me with my hoody an (sic) I raised the gun an (sic) he saw it and *tried* to get out the car so I fired again while he was getting out in the back an (sic) he took off running an (sic) I got out an (sic) he ran in a truck an (sic) I went to check on him then I got back into the car an (sic) pulled off an (sic) went to my grandparents house because I didn't know what to do."

The writer uses the verbs of interrupted action **started** and **tried** numerous times in the statement. But what interrupted the action? The writer shooting Jimmy and Snoot. Snoot tried to fight the writer, but this action was interrupted when the writer raised his gun to shoot Snoot again. Snoot then tried get out of the car, but was shot by the writer again. Snoot did finally escape the car to only be hit by a truck. Karma, man!

In my opinion, this statement is truthful. The writer uses verbs of interrupted action, but he then gives the reason for the interruption. If someone is being deceptive, they will use the verbs of interrupted action but will not explain what interrupted the action. They hope you will fill in the blanks, so they don't have to.

Passive Voice versus Active Voice

Good writers use active voice because it brings the action closer to the actor. Conversely, passive voice put distance between the actor and the action.

For example, "Mad Dog shot the gun" versus "The gun was shot by Mad Dog." The first sentence shows Mad Dog shooting the gun, whereas the second creates distance between the gun and Mad Dog's action.

If someone has done something they are not proud of or will get them in trouble, they will use passive voice.

For example, if an employee misses a project deadline and you ask the employee about the task's status, the employee can answer in the active voice ("I didn't complete the task on time") or passive voice ("The task was not completed on time" or "The task was not completed on time by me"). The active voice takes ownership and the passive does not. The passive voice creates separation between the uncompleted task and the employee. Additionally, it can hide the identity of the person who failed to complete the task.

The following sentence taken from a statement given by the live-in boyfriend in a sexual assault investigation combines the verb of uncompleted action and passive voice.

"The only thing I can think of is that I try (interrupted action) to be a real father to Joann, and that means that sometimes punishment is given to her" (passive voice).

So, the boyfriend tries to be a real father, and in his mind that means punishing the daughter, Joann. But he doesn't want to admit that he punishes her, so he uses the passive-voice verb, "punishment is given to her." The active-voice verb would be "I punish her," but that directly links him to the act of punishment.

Remember, passive voice creates distance between the actor and the action.

Six Verbs that Indicate Deception

There are six verbs that I have found to be present in most deceptive statements. They are:

- Realized
- Noticed
- Decided
- Determined
- Managed
- Glanced

I know what you're thinking, *But Frank, I use these verbs all the time and I'm not deceptive*. I agree. I use them also. But I have found that these verbs pop up often when someone wants to be deceptive and misleading.

When we examine what these verbs mean, it becomes clearer how they are used in deceptive language.

Realized means that something just dawned on you. This realization comes as a surprise to you. If someone uses "realized" in connection with something that is not unusual or out of the ordinary, I would question that word usage. Why did they "realize" something that should be, under normal circumstances, expected? Realized is used to distance the writer/speaker from something or some action.

Noticed indicates you saw something but did not attribute any significance or weight to what you saw. Noticed is almost like an afterthought and the writer/speaker is downplaying their connection with the incident or item. If someone says they saw the car accident, they are now a witness, as opposed to, someone who noticed the accident. Their connection to the accident and the possibility of becoming a witness is greatly lessened by using noticed.

Decided and **determined** indicates a decision was made, either through collaboration with another individual or by weighing all the pertinent factors and deciding on a course of action. Whenever I see decided or determined in a statement, I want to know who was involved in the decision or determination and how was it decided. I also want to explore what factors were considered when making the decision.

Managed indicates a level of difficulty accomplishing something. Consider the following two sentences: "I went into my bedroom" versus "I managed to get into my bedroom." Obviously, the first sentence indicates no difficulty, whereas the second does. Whenever someone uses managed to describe how they did something, ask why it was difficult or what caused the difficulty.

Glanced indicates you saw something, but barely. Like noticed, glanced downplays what you saw and how much you saw. It is a way to minimize your connection with something or some action.

As you can see, verbs are the most dynamic and versatile part of our language and provide insight into what someone is saying, thinking, and doing.

Quick Tips:

1. Rule of Thumb: the past is the past and the present is the present. Past-tense verbs should be used to describe past events and present-tense verbs to describe current events. If past-tense and present-tense verbs are used to describe a past event, the statement is deceptive.

Remember the missing person exception!

2. Identify all verbs of communication (talked, chatted, discussed, said) and verbs of masked communication (met for lunch, watched TV, drove).

3. Look for verbs of interrupted action (started, began, initiated).

4. Active voice takes ownership of actions. Passive voice distances one from ownership of actions.

5. Look for the six verbs that indicate deception (realized, noticed, decided, determined, managed, glanced).

CHAPTER 11:

Pronouns

Pronouns tell us so much about each other. Pronouns tell us what and who is important in our lives. We show the world what we own and possess through the use of pronouns. You can tell who are couples with pronouns. Pronouns also give us insight to the type of relationship that exists and if it is a strained relationship or not. Yes, pronouns are very interesting.

Pronouns are words that stand in for nouns. There are three types of pronouns. They are:

1. First person—I, me, my, we, us

2. Second person—you

3. Third person—he, him, she, her, they, them, it

In Deceptive Language Analysis, I prefer to think of pronouns in terms of personal and possessive. Personal pronouns (I, you, he, she, we, they) refer to people, animals, and objects. Possessive pronouns (my, our, yours, his, hers, theirs) refer to ownership or possession of something or someone.

The use of a fist person personal pronoun such as I indicates commitment to the action or activity on the part of the speaker or writer. An absence of the first-person pronoun may indicate a distancing from the action or activity.

More significant is a shift from the first person I to the second person you. I indicates something you did or have done. You indicates what someone else did or has done. It also may indicate that the writer is distancing themselves from the action to evade personal responsibility. For example: "So, I decided not to review each and every report. You get tired after a twelve-hour shift and you just want to go home and rest."

In this example, the speaker admits to not fulfilling his duties of reviewing all of the reports, but distances himself from his reasons for not completing his job by using the second-person pronoun you instead of the first-person pronoun I. He could have easily and more truthfully have said this: "So, I decided not to review each and every report. I was tired after a twelve-hour shift and I just wanted to go home and rest."

In this sentence, the speaker is taking full responsibility for his actions and the reasons for not completing his job.

Let's look at an example where there is an absence of first-person pronouns. Assume you are a restaurant owner and you are interviewing candidates for the position of Sous Chef and you ask the following question:

Q: "What were your duties as a Sous Chef at your last job?"

A: "Well, the usual things. You know, you help with the kitchen prep, you help the chef with menu planning, you help with the cooking."

Did the applicant tell you what he did at his last job? Hardly. The applicant did not take ownership of anything he described as his duties from the last job. The use of the second-person pronoun you deceptively indicates the applicant did these activities at the last job while never saying he or she did these duties.

Compare these answers:

A: "Well, the usual things. You know, you help with the kitchen prep, you help the chef with menu planning, you help with the cooking."

versus

A: "Well, the usual things. You know, I helped with the kitchen prep, I helped the chef with menu planning, I helped with the cooking."

Which sounds more believable? The first answer distances the applicant from these actions, whereas the second answer takes full ownership of the answer. Additionally, the first answer uses the present-tense verb help versus the past-tense verb helped. As we discussed earlier, the use of present-tense verbs to describe past events strongly indicates deception.

The Use of We

The personal pronoun we may indicate that a relationship exists between people. We go on trips together, we eat together, we do activities together. The use of we indicates a consent to do things together.

Compare the following sentences:

"He took me into the woods."

versus

"We went into the woods."

Which sentence indicates consent and a relationship? The first obviously shows a lack of consent and the second reflects an agreement to go into the woods together.

In a sexual assault cases such as a date rape, the use of the personal pronoun we is expected at the outset of the statement, but when things turn sour, the we should disappear and be replaced with he and I.

Let's look at the pronouns in the following statement, where a college student was visiting a fraternity house on campus.

"Jed came over and started to massage *my* shoulders. *He* then asked me if *I* wanted to see the house. *I* said ok so *we* went inside. *We* went through the kitchen and then down the hall to the foyer to a room that had a piano. *We* stayed in that room for about 15 minutes. *We* talked and *I* played the piano. *He* said do you want to see the upstairs, so *I* said alright. *We* went upstairs and then *he* took *me* to Stan's bedroom. *He* then started kissing *me*. While *we* were kissing *we* made our way to the bed and laid down. *We* kissed for a couple of minutes and *he* started to unbutton *my* blouse. Then *he* pulled *my* blouse off, undid *my* bra and took it off. *He* then undid *my* pants. *I* started feeling uncomfortable and tried to button them back up. *I* said *I* would like to go back to the party. *I* started to sit up and *he* said no the party is here. *My* heart was pounding, and *I* kept trying to get up and *he* kept pushing *me* down. *I* said no, no, *I* want to go. *He* then started to finger *me*, and *I* went limp. *He* said so that's the way you're going to be now. *He* got off *me* and *I* got up and got dressed. *I* went to the door, opened it to leave and *he* shut the light off and then grabbed *me* around the neck and pulled *me* back on the bed. *I* pulled away and screamed loud. *He* pushed *my* head into the bed so *I* couldn't scream. *He* twisted *my* neck. *He* said, "*I* swear to God I'll break *your* fucking neck, now take *your* pants off." *I* said no. *He* said, "*I'll* kill *you* kill *you*, drop *you* in a body bag in Philly and no one would ever know." *He* pulled *my* pants off. *I* was just crying and saying no, please don't hurt *me*. *He* punched *me* about four times. *I* told him *I* couldn't breathe. *He* then rolled *me* on my back, and *I* felt him push *his* penis against *me*. Then *he* put it in *me,* and *I* started to cry, oh God, oh God."

Everything is going well in the above statement until Jed pulled her blouse off. The victim used the pronoun we numerous times until things started going too far. After that point in the statement, the pronoun we disappears and is replaced with he and I. At that point, the consent was gone, as was the pronoun we. They were no longer engaged in an agreed-upon activity together.

Here are a couple of additional thoughts on this statement.

First, this is a heartbreakingly sad statement. When I read it, my heart goes out to the victim. I believe this statement is truthful because of the balance of the statement and the amount of unique sensory detail and spatial detail in the incident box of the statement.

Second, I hope something dreadful happened to Jed, say like a brain tumor. He is a true predator.

Shifting Pronouns

Possessive pronouns indicate ownership of objects and the closeness of our relationship with others. If you refer to **your** car as **my car**, then you are claiming ownership of your car. If you refer to your car as **the** car, well, maybe you don't really consider it your car. You subconsciously don't claim ownership of the car. The rule of thumb is if the possessive pronoun disappears, then the writer/speaker is distancing themselves from the object, person, or place.

Let's look at a couple of examples. The first is a statement made by the alleged victim of a house arson.

I left *my* house right after breakfast to join my friends at the track for the day. I drove back to *my* house, made a few phone calls, then went out to dinner with Stan Thompson. Stan dropped me off at *my* house around 10:00. After I changed my clothes, I left *the house* to spend the night at my cousin Tom's. Around midnight we heard fire engines and got up to see what was going on.

In the first three lines of the statement, he refers to his house as my house. But in line three, it changes to the house. He appears to be distancing himself from the ownership of the house. In the next line, the house is on fire.

The question you are asking yourself is why did the personal pronouns referring to his house change? You probably suspect why.

The alleged victim had a gambling problem. He liked to play the ponies. He was deeply in debt and going through a nasty divorce. His life was a slow-moving train wreck. He needed money, so he decided to burn down his house in order to collect the insurance money. The arson investigator quickly suspected the victim of being the arsonist, conducted a good interview, and the victim admitted to the arson.

The next statement was given by Susan Smith following her confession of murdering her two children.

"When I was at John D. Long Lake, I had never felt so scared and unsure as I did then. I wanted to end my life so bad and was in *my car* ready to go down that ramp into the water, and I did go part way, but I stopped. I went again and stopped. I then got out of *the car* and stood by *the car* a nervous wreck."

Once again, the possessive pronoun "my car" changes to "the car" when she finally lets her car roll into the lake and her children drown. When she made that decision, she subconsciously gave up ownership of the car. She wanted distance from it and what she had done.

The last statement we'll look at is given by a husband who claimed his wife drowned while they were out on boating.

My wife and I left home about 9 a.m. and went to the marina where we keep *our boat*. *My wife* and I left the marina in *the boat* at 10:30 a.m. I picked up some fuel and odd and ends at the boat store then she and I headed for Captain's Cove, about 5 miles out. Arriving around 11:30 a.m. I anchored *the boat* and then *my wife* and I started to swim. It was about 11:50 when I noticed that *Sandi* was nowhere to be found.

Oh boy, where do we start?

He uses the possessive pronoun "our boat" in the first sentence, but changes it to "the boat" and continues to use that reference throughout the remainder of the statement. Like the previous house-arson statement, the husband changes the possessive pronoun "my boat" to "the boat" thus gives up possession of his boat in the statement. Why the change?

More interesting, though, is how he refers to his spouse. He consistently refers to her as "my wife" up to the time when he realizes she is missing. He then shifts his reference to her from "my wife" to "Sandi." Experience has shown that perpetrators of familial violence have a difficult time admitting to harming a family member. By shifting from the possessive pronoun "my wife" to "Sandi," he distances himself from his familial ties to his wife.

One other thing that should also jump out is the change in references to time. As we discussed in the chapter 7, we always look for any changes in how time is referenced.

Throughout the statement, the husband always referred to time using a.m. In lines one, two, and four, he referenced time using a.m., but in the last line of the statement it changes to just 11:50. This also coincided with the moment of most tension in the statement, when his wife disappeared.

The husband later admitted to drowning his wife and using odds and ends, like the extra anchor and a length of nylon rope he purchased at the boat store to weigh down her body.

Pronouns may seem like a small part of our vocabulary, but if you know what to look and listen for they can tell you a lot about the person you are talking to.

Quick Tips

1. There are three types of pronouns. They are:

First person—I, me, my, we, us

Second person—you

Third person—he, him, she, her, they, them, it

2. Use of the first-person singular pronoun I reflects commitment to an action or activity by the speaker/writer.
3. Use of the second-person singular pronoun you indicates a lack of commitment to action or activity by the speaker/writer.
4. The first-person plural pronoun we indicates a relationship exist or there exists agreement to an action or activity. If the agreement or relationship is strained or breached, we will likely be replaced with he/she and I or they.

5. Possessive pronouns (me, my, our, your, his, hers, theirs) Disappearance of possessive pronouns may suggest the speaker/writer is distancing himself from the person, objects, or place. Example my house > the house, my car > the car.

CHAPTER 12:

Intensifiers, Minimizers, and Time Jumps

When we communicate, we are always doing three things: Conveying information; trying to convince someone; or a combination of the two.

If someone just gives you the facts, down and dirty, without a lot of hyperbole, the chances are they are telling the truth. They are not trying to convince or entertain you. They are just conveying information.

If someone uses intensifiers and minimizers to tell the same story, they may be telling the truth and trying to be entertaining. Or they may be being deceptive and trying to convince you that they are being truthful.

Adverbs modify verbs, adjectives, and other adverbs. They can broaden and limit, intensify, or minimize. For example, quickly ran is an intensifying adverb/verb, while just talked is a minimizing adverb/verb, unusually loud is an intensifying adverb/adjective, and always patiently is an intensifying adverb/adverb.

As you can see, it gets to be a bit confusing. Because of this, I prefer to think in terms of intensifiers and minimizers.

Intensifiers

Intensifiers are adverbs that make a word more. Some examples of intensifiers are:

- very
- really
- always
- quite
- truthfully
- honestly
- again
- still
- finally

If the speaker invokes God, he or she is using an intensifier. If they say, "Honest to god," "I swear on a stack of bibles," or "Hand to God," beware. They are trying to convince you.

If the speaker also tells you he/she is being truthful, watch out. If they say things like, "to be honest with you", to tell you the truth", "Honestly", "Truthfully", they are trying to convince you more than convey information.

It reminds me of advice my dad gave me years ago. He said, "If someone tells you how honest they are, immediately put your hand on your wallet."

I realize that there will always be room for some hyperbole. It makes language more interesting and entertaining. Without intensifiers, President Trump's tweets would have been half as long but much less entertaining.

Think of a salesman doing a hard sell. He will use intensifiers to tell how great his product or service is. Maybe their product or service is the best, really great, in a league of its own, but when I hear the use of too many intensifiers, my BS antenna goes up.

When it comes to deceptive language, intensifiers show up more often than not.

Minimizing Adverbs

Minimizers adverbs are used when someone wants to downplay their culpability or distance themselves from an unpleasant action or event.

Some examples off minimizing adverbs are:

- only
- just
- simply
- yet
- barely
- or phrases such as, not too much and hardly any

Think of the co-worker who has gossiped about you to your boss. When called upon to answer for her actions, she says, "I simply repeated what I had heard others say." Did she simply repeat rumors, or did she editorialize or start the initial rumor? By using the word simply, she is minimizing her actions.

The following is a letter sent by a man named Joshua, the owner of a deer-processing company. For those unfamiliar with deer processing, when a hunter has killed and field dressed a deer, they can either butcher it themselves or take it to a deer-processing company where it will be butchered and packaged for the hunter.

Unfortunately, Joshua's company did not obtain the proper licenses to process deer, and this letter is Joshua's mea culpa to the county board. Pay particular attention to the intensifiers and minimizers Joshua uses. (The intensifiers and minimizers are in bold italics.)

Jan 14ᵗʰ, 2003

Joshua XXXX

To whom it may concern, I wish to *simply* say that I meant no harm and was unaware of *99%* of the wrong that I've committed. If *all* these things I have done are illegal, *as god as my witness,* I wasn't aware of it. If I were making *a lot of money* at the deer cooler, I wouldn't have another *full-time* job and *2 other* businesses. I run XXX Deer cooler *mostly* because I enjoy it, the people, wild stories - because *God knows I basically* break even each season on this particular business (taxes show it). Call the customers and ask them about my service and what kind of person I am - look at my prices - I turn out, *nearly* the best quality at the *lowest* price around!! I'm not the *brightest* businessman in town, but I am one of the *hardest* workers you will ever meet. I've got 3 beautiful kids, a new house, a strong supportive family, and *a firm belief in God.* So *god* hears me tell you, that what I say *is honest.* And I assure you all, that I will become aware of and *fully* adhere to *every* rule that I must follow, and any information that you need in the future - I will provide.

Thanks for listening.

Joshua XXXX

owner of XXXX Deer Cooler

Joshua starts by telling us that he "simply" meant no harm and "was unaware of 99% of the wrong I've committed." Obviously, Joshua is attempting to minimize his culpability. I suspect he may have been aware of few more percent than he is claiming.

Then he drags God into by saying "If all these things I have done are illegal, as god as my witness, I wasn't aware of it." Here he is trying to convince, not convey information.

Joshua then tells us that he isn't making any money on this business venture ("If I were making a lot of money at the deer cooler, I wouldn't have another full time job and 2 other businesses") and only runs the company so he can socialize with the hunters and hear their wild stories ("I run XXX deer cooler mostly because I enjoy it, the people, wild stories—because God knows I basically break even each season on this particular business (taxes show it.")). Not sure that's a defense I would want to use in court. "Your Honor, I know I broke the law, but I didn't make any money and I was helping wayward deer hunters." He once again invokes the good lord as his witness of his business's finances.

Even though Joshua isn't making any money, he wants us to know that the Deer Cooler produces "nearly the best quality at the lowest price around!!" He would not be so presumptuous to claim to be the best quality, he humble brags that he produces "nearly the best quality." I like that.

Joshua rounds the last turn by calling out the Almighty a couple of times and tells us how honest he is. All right everyone, hands on wallets.

He finishes by assuring us he has learned from his wicked ways and will "fully adhere to every rule I must follow."

Time Jumps

When someone wants to conceal their actions or something that occurred, they will use what I call a time jump.

Time jumps are adverbs used to move a story along. If someone says, "I packed my bags and then went to the airport," they are using the time jump "then" to cover the time and activities that took place between finishing packing their bags and leaving for the airport.

This is not saying that every time jump is an indication of nefarious behavior. It just moves the story ahead in time, but it can be used to conceal events or actions.

Consider this: How many times will someone say, "Hold on, go back and tell me what you did after you packed your bag." Almost never, because it feels awkward and pushy. But let's say that the house where you packed your bag burned down after you left for the airport. Then we may want to get more specific about everything done after packing the bag and before leaving for the airport.

Some of the most common text bridges are:

- after that
- the next thing I knew
- later on
- afterward
- shortly thereafter
- consequently
- however
- next
- while
- even though
- then
- finally
- before
- so
- as
- once
- later

Let's take a look at a statement using time jumps.

Question: Please describe your actions on January 19, 2009, and January 20, 2009.

I got up about 10:00 AM. I ***then*** went to the country

house + removed a hot water heater. I ***then*** took the

hot water heater to 2544 Dixie Farms Rd. My wifes

house about 4:00 PM. I ***then*** started removeing +

reinstalling the hot water heater. I got through with

the installation about 9:00. I ***then*** had some drinks

with my wife + helped gather the children. ***Then***

about 9 or 10 PM we started getting ready for bed.

Then about 1:00 AM 1:45 AM the phone started

ringing. Don't remember who. I finally woke up + my

sister was in panic. So I made my way to her house

got there about 2:30 we ***then*** left for Millard (Dale,

Shauna, Nece, Lancy and me) at about 3:30 4:00).

This is an alibi statement, and the writer is trying to account for his activities on the day his mother was murdered.

In his statement, the writer's time jump of choice is ***then***. He uses it over and over. He wants to move the story along with no elaboration.

There are other interesting aspects of this statement.

The writer uses the verb of uncompleted action "started" three times.

Once when he "started removeing + reinstalling the hot water heater."

The second is when "we started getting ready for bed."

The third time is when "the phone started ringing."

The writer uses the equivocation "about" every time he references time.

The writer's timeline is inconsistent. He uses four lines to cover six hours (10:00 a.m. to 4:00 p.m.). He then uses three lines to cover five hours (4:00 p.m. to 9:00 p.m.). The pace changes for the rest of the statement (two lines to cover one hour). He is vague concerning his activities for the day up to "9:00." After that, he tightens up his timeline later in the night.

He consistently uses a.m. and p.m. until "9:00," when he finished the installation of the hot water heater. "Then about 9 or 10 p.m. we started getting ready for bed." So there is an inconsistency with his timeline here.

The last thing he uses is an equivocation when he says, "So I made my way to her house." What does that mean? And if his sister is "in panic" over the death of their mother, the writer seems rather sanguine about the situation. Maybe the news of his mother's death isn't that surprising for him.

If I were interviewing the writer, we would have a long conversation.

Casey Anthony Statement

Almost everyone recalls Casey Anthony, the mother of the murdered three-year-old girl, Caylee Anthony. Contrary to popular belief, Caylee Anthony went missing on Monday, June 9, 2008, not, as widely reported in the media, on June 15, 2008.

Cindy Anthony, Casey Anthony's mother, called 911 to report Caylee missing on July 15, 2008. Cindy hadn't seen Caylee for weeks and Casey gave several contradictory answers to Caylee's whereabouts when questioned by Cindy. Additionally, when Casey's car was retrieved from the impound lot, the trunk smelled like body decomposition which made Casey's parents suspicious.

The following is Casey Anthony's statement given to the police. Read it and see what you think. We will then analyze it for balance and look at intensifiers, minimizers, time jumps, and other interesting items.

On Monday, June 9, 2008, between 9 am and 1 pm, I, Casey Anthony, took my daughter, Caylee Marie Anthony, to her nanny's apartment. Caylee will be 3 years old on August 9, 2008. She was born on August 9, 2005. Caylee is about 3 feet tall, white female, with shoulder-length, light brown hair. She has dark hazel eyes (brown/green), and a small birthmark on her left shoulder. On the day of her disappearance, Caylee was wearing a pink shirt, with jean shorts, white sneakers, and her hair was pulled back in a ponytail. On Monday, June 9, 2008, between 9 am and 1 pm, I took Caylee to the Sawgrass Apartments, located on Conway Rd. Caylee's nanny, Zenaida Fernandez-Gonzalez, has watched her for the past year and a half, to two years. Zenaida is twenty-five years old and is from New York. She is roughly 5 for 7 inches tall, 140 pounds. She has dark brown, curly hair, and brown eyes. Zenaida's birthday is in September. I met Zenaida, through a mutual friend, Jeffrey Michael Hopkins. She has watched his son, Zachary Hopkins, for about 6 months to a year. I met Zenaida in 2004, around Christmas. On the date listed above, June 9, 2008, I proceeded to head to my place of employment, Universal Studios Orlando. I have worked at Universal for over four years since June of 2004. I left work around 5 pm, went back to the apartments to pick up my daughter. However, after reaching the apartment, I realized that neither Zenaida, Caylee, or either of her two roommates were home. I have briefly met Raquel Farrell, and Jennifer Rosa on various occasions. After calling Zenaida to see where she and Caylee were, and when they were coming home, I waited outside of the apartment. I had called Zenaida earlier that morning, prior to bringing Caylee over for the afternoon. When I called her that afternoon, her phone was no longer in service. Two hours passed, and around 7 pm, I left the apartment, headed to familiar places that Zenaida would go with Caylee. One of Caylee's favorite places is Jay Blanchard Park. I spent the rest of the evening pacing and worrying at one of the few places I felt "at home", my boyfriend Anthony Lozzaro's apartment. For the past four weeks, since Caylee's disappearance, I have stayed at Anthony's apartment in Sutton Place. I have spent every day, since Monday, June 9, 2008, looking for my daughter. I have lied and stolen from friends and family, to do whatever I could by any means, to find my daughter. I avoided calling the police, or even notifying my own family out of fear. I have been, and still am afraid of what has, or may happen too Caylee. I have not had any contact with Zenaida since Thursday, June 12, 2008. I received a quick call from Zenaida. Not once have I been able to ask her for my daughter or gain any information on where I can find her. Every day, I have gone to malls, parks, any place I could remember Zenaida taking Caylee. I have gone out, and tried to find any information about Caylee, or Zenaida, whether by going to a popular bar, or restaurant. I have contacted Jeff Hopkins on several occasions to see if he had heard from or seen Zenaida. Jeff currently lives in Jacksonville, Florida.

On Tuesday, July 15, 2008, around 12 pm, I received a phone call from my daughter, Caylee. Today was the first day I have heard her voice in over 4 weeks. I'm afraid of what Caylee is going through. After 31 days, I know that the only thing that matters is getting my daughter back. With many and all attempts to contact Zenaida, and within the one short conversation, on June 12, 2008, I was never able to check on the status or the well-being of my daughter. Zenaida never made an attempt to explain why Caylee is no longer in Orlando, or if she is ever going to bring her home.

The statement is 45 lines long. The PIE is as follows:

P—17 ÷ 45 = 38%

I—9 ÷ 45 = 20%

E—19 ÷ 45 = 42%

Anthony's statement is wildly out of balance.

In my opinion, the incident box starts on line eighteen with "However, after reaching the apartment, I realized that neither Zenaida, Caylee, or either of her two roommates were home" and it ends with, "One of Caylee's favorite places is Jay Blanchard Park." Out of the entire statement, Anthony only dedicates twenty percent to addressing the disappearance of her daughter thirty-seven days earlier!

The prologue and epilogue are far longer and contain mainly extraneous information. Like Susan Smith, Anthony provides details in an effort to appear cooperative, but most of it is general in nature and is irrelevant for the purpose of finding out what happened to Caylee.

Let's use DLA on her statement.

Anthony starts her statement with the equivocation, "between 9 a.m. and 1 p.m." for when she drops her daughter, Caylee, off at the nanny's apartment. She repeats this again later in the statement. Anthony gives herself a four-hour window for dropping off her daughter. She says that after dropping Caylee off, she "proceeded to place of employment, Universal Studios Orlando." "Proceeded to" is an verb of uncompleted action. Did she go to work or not?

Anthony states, "I left work around 5 p.m., and went to the apartment to pick up my daughter." So, if Anthony dropped off Caylee at 1:00 p.m., then went to work but leaves work at 5:00 p.m., that means she is working less than four hours a day. But if she worked a full shift, the 9:00 a.m. drop-off time would make more sense. Why does she give herself a four-hour time block for dropping off Caylee? As some will remember, Anthony did not work at Universal Studios Orlando. She was lying. She was building an alibi.

The epilogue is the longest part of the statement and it contains most of the intensifiers and minimizers and time jumps. This is where Anthony tries to convince the reader that she was doing everything humanly possible to find Caylee. Everything except notifying the police or her family.

Some examples of intensifiers and minimizers Casey Anthony used are:

"I spent the rest of the evening pacing and worrying at one of the few places I felt 'at home,' my boyfriend Anthony Lozzaro's apartment. For the past four weeks, since Caylee's disappearance, I have stayed at Anthony's apartment in Sutton Place. I have spent every day, (intensifier) since Monday, June 9, 2008, looking for my daughter. II have lied and stolen (unusual use of verbs. Why lie and steal from friends and family?) from friends and family, to do whatever I could, by any means, (intensifier) to find my daughter. I avoided calling the police (Why?), or even notifying (minimizer) my own family out of fear (fear of what?). I have been, and still am afraid (emotion) of what has or may happen to Caylee. (So afraid that she doesn't tell anyone or obtain help in finder her daughter!). I have not (negation) had any contact with Zenaida since Thursday, June 12, 2008. I received a quick (minimizer) call from Zenaida. Not once (negation) have I been able to ask her for my daughter or gain any (minimizer) information on where I can find her. Every day, (intensifier) I have gone to malls, parks, any (intensifier) place I could remember Zenaida taking Caylee. I have gone out and tried (verb of uncompleted action) to find any information about Caylee, or Zenaida, whether by going to a popular bar, or restaurant. I have contacted Jeff Hopkins on several occasions (intensifier and shows a lack of urgency) to see if he had heard from or seen Zenaida. Jeff currently lives in Jacksonville, Florida.

On Tuesday, July 15, 2008, around 12 p.m., I received a phone call from my daughter, Caylee. Today was the first (intensifier) day I have heard her voice in over four weeks. I'm afraid of what Caylee is going through. After thirty-one days, (It was actually thirty-seven days, but who's counting?) I know that the only thing that matters (intensifier) is getting my daughter back. With many and all (intensifier) attempts (verb of uncompleted action) to contact Zenaida, and within the one short (minimizer) conversation, on June 12, 2008, I was never (negation) able to check on the status or the well-being of my daughter. Zenaida never (negation) made an attempt to explain why Caylee is no longer in Orlando, (how does she know they are not in Orlando any longer?) or if she is ever going to bring her home."

Like O.J. Simpson looking for the killers on America's golf courses, Anthony was determined to find her daughter without the assistance of the people with the most experience in missing-persons investigations, law enforcement. She writes, "I avoided calling the police, or even notifying my own family out of fear." Why? What was she afraid of? She says she searched malls and parks where Zenaida took Caylee, but also says, "I have gone out, and tried to find any information about Caylee, or Zenaida, whether by going to a popular bar, or restaurant." So, did Zenaida and Caylee frequent popular bars and restaurants in the Orlando area? This is a prime example of extraneous information. She is justifying why she had been seen partying at bars and restaurants in the Orlando area while her daughter is missing.

Another strange thing she says is, "I have lied and stolen from friends and family, to do whatever I could by any means, to find my daughter." Why did she feel compelled to lie and steal from her friends and family while searching for Caylee?

Anthony contradicts herself concerning her contacts with Zenaida and Caylee. In the last paragraph of the epilogue, Anthony says she received a phone call on July 15, 2008, around 12 p.m. from Caylee, but later in the same paragraph contradicts herself by saying she had one contact with Zenaida on June 12, 2008 and "was never able to check on the status or the well-being of my daughter." She just said she had a phone call from Caylee. Did she not ask Caylee about her well-being and her location? Of course not, because the phone call did not happen. Anthony is only giving this statement to the police because her mother contacted the police, not her. I assume she wants the police to think this is still a missing child case and not a homicide.

Of course, Casey Anthony was full of crap and the statement is as deceptive as you think. Over the course of the investigation and her trial, her story changed several times. It became apparent that Anthony was responsible for the disappearance of Caylee, if not her death. But, as what happens all too often in our judicial system, her lawyers raised enough reasonable doubt to obtain a not-guilty verdict.

In closing, if someone uses a lot of intensifiers, minimizers, and time jumps, they are probably trying to convince you more than convey truthful information.

Quick Tips

1. Intensifiers—very, really, honestly—used to convince more than convey information

2. Minimizers—only, just, simply, basically—used to downplay actions or activities.

3. Time Jumps—then, later, after, next—used to move the story along and jump over details in the story.

4. Use of extreme intensifiers such as "Honest to god," " I swear on a stack of bibles," or "On my child's life" are sure signs the speaker/writer is more interested in convincing you of their innocence than conveying pertinent information.

CHAPTER 13:

Amplification Questions

At this point, I've shown you how to identify the verbal tricks people use to fool and deceive. So what to do with all of this newfound knowledge? Put it to use, of course. And we do that by asking questions.

There are two ways to ask a question, closed end and open-end questions.

Close end questions are questions answered with a yes or no. They provide little or no elaboration. They can be leading and are used to validate the premise of a question. By asking close ended questions, the opportunity for leakage, i.e., someone inadvertently revealing information that can be used for further questioning, is lost.

Close end questions will start with:

"Do you agree…."

"Is it not true…."

"Wouldn't you agree…."

"Will you agree that…."

On the other hand, open end questions seek elaboration. They are worded in a way that causes the interviewee to provide more detail and expound freely about the subject at hand.

Open end questions will start with the 5Ws and How:

"How did this occur?"

"What do you remember about ….?"

"When did you realize …?"

"Where were you when ….?"

"Who was with you when….?"

"Why….?"

They can also start with:

"Tell me about…"

"Please explain."

"You said…."

I want to provide a word of warning about using "Why" in an open-end question. When people are asked why they did or said something, they usually become defensive. Why sounds accusatory. Any why question can be reworded to soften the tenor of the questioning. Instead of asking "Why did you do that?", ask, "What caused you to do that?". The question, "Why did you do that?", demands an accounting for your actions and your justification for your actions. The second question, "What caused you to do that?", subtle sends the message that there are reasons for their actions. The interviewee won't feel compelled to defend their actions. The conversation will flow more freely and isn't that the whole purpose of an interview? Remember, an interview is just a conversation with a direction.

There may come a time when you want to create stress during an interview and using a why question may be appropriate. I've occasionally used why questions to ramp up the stress level in tense interviews in hopes of obtaining an admission from the interviewee. These admissions are usually small but can be important. The admission may the first step in moving the interviewee from uncooperative to cooperative.

Questions can also be used to persuade. I always start my interviews by telling the interviewee that I need their help and then tell them what I want to talk to them about. By asking them for their help, I am tapping in the human psyche which make us want to be helpful or at least appear to be helpful. I also ask for their cooperation. If at any time they become uncooperative, I will remind them that they said they would be helpful and cooperative. This will put pressure on them to be consistent with their words and action. In his book, "Influence: The Psychology of Persuasion", Dr. Robert Cialdini found that people strive to act consistent with their words. If someone agrees to do something, they inherently try to be consistent with this commitment. That is why obtaining their commitment to cooperate is so powerful.

Amplification questions are used to get clarification on what a person said or wrote. If posed in the right way, amplification questions will cause the person to explain why he/she chose the words they used and why they answered the way they did. Amplification questions are always open ended.

For example, if someone uses verbs like decided, noticed, or glanced, simply ask, "Tell me more about that." Now the person is forced to provide more information, which, if they are trying to deceive you, they definitely do not want to do.

Other questions you can ask are:

- "Why did you chose to refer to (person, place, item, situation) as that?"
- "What did you mean when you said _____?"
- "What did you do next?"
- "How was this decided?"
- "What factors did you consider when making this decision?"

When someone is in a position where they should possess certain information but continues to say they don't know, ask, "Why don't you know this?"

All of these questions will force the person to give additional information. The more someone talks, the more they give away regarding their mindset and motivations. Even if they refuse to answer the question, their refusal tells you that they are being deceptive. At that point, you just have to decide if you want to pursue further interactions with this person.

People have a wide variety of reasons why they deceive. Some reasons are nefarious. Some are out of shame and embarrassment. Sometimes they are trying to protect someone. That's why I don't try to catch them in The Big Lie. By asking good amplification questions, they will expose themselves, and now you know what to look for when they do.

EPILOGUE:

Mercenary versus Missionary

As an FBI Special Agent, I investigated a wide variety of perpetrators for various crimes. In the FBI, we called perpetrators "subjects." Some were smart, some were dumb, some were evil, and some were extremely misguided.

I used whatever tools were necessary to make my case in preparation for prosecution. One of the most potent tools I had in my toolbox was my ability to talk to people. Because of my blue-collar upbringing, I was able to relate to a lot of the people I investigated. I grew up with people just like them. If the coin flip in my life had gone a different way, I may have ended up in similar situations.

Anyway, I always tried to get confessions from my subject.

The mercenary in me wanted a confession to assure a conviction. By the time I interviewed the subject of my case, I had gathered sufficient evidence to charge them already. A confession was icing on the cake, and would usually ensure a plea deal.

The missionary in me wanted a confession because I could then tell the prosecutor that the subject had taken responsibility for their actions. It would open the door for a lower sentence and the opportunity to further cooperate if there were other subjects in the case.

In the business world, it is no different.

In sales or negotiations, the mercenary in us wants to close the sale no matter what or get the best deal possible in negotiations. Some people will use deceptive language to do this.

The missionary in you wants to serve your client by selling them a product or service that will benefit them or their business. In negotiations, you want to reach an agreement that is mutually beneficial for all involved parties.

The only way to strike the balance between the mercenary and the missionary is to limit the use of deceptive language.

Knowing and understanding DLA will keep you from venturing into the seductive field of deceptive language that beckons us. Your answers will be clear and with little extraneous information. You will also know when you are dealing with someone who is deceptive.

Always convey information that is convincing instead of trying to convince.

The avoidance of deceptive language will make your communications more authentic. People like and trust authentic people. People buy from authentic people.

Subjects confess to people they trust, and trust can only be achieved by being authentic.

I never had to worry about a false confession because I didn't try to fool people by using deception. I was authentic, I listened with curiosity, and I invested in building rapport.

If you do those three things, you will usually achieve what you want and get the proper result.

Unfortunately, I can't say the same for all of my FBI brethren. As I write this, more evidence continues to come to light that corrupt FBI officials perpetrated a fraud on the American people by pushing the false Russian Collusion hoax and tried to frame Lieutenant General Michael Flynn.

It appears that Director James Comey, Deputy Director Andrew McCabe, Assistant Director Bill Preistap, Deputy Assistant Director Peter Strzok, and

FBI General Counsel Lisa Page were involved in a plan to ensnare Flynn in a false statement trap with the goal of either criminally charging him or getting him fired from his position as White House National Security Director. Additionally, documents were falsified and lies told to the FISA Court to illegally spy on Carter Page, a low-level Trump campaign advisor and unknown others in the Trump Administration in furtherance of the bogus Russian Collusion hoax.

As a retired FBI agent, I can assure everyone that the FBI should be concerned with getting to the truth, not tricking someone into lying. Nor should they ever be concerned with getting anyone fired. If someone committed a crime, it is their job to follow the evidence and present it to the federal prosecutors and let them decide to prosecute or not. That alone tells me that their scheme was bogus.

These officials lost their way. They were dominated by their mercenary side. Their missionary side was nowhere in sight.

They were only concerned with protecting themselves or gaining some advantage for future use.

They are a stain on the FBI and, unfortunately, I believe this is just the tip of the iceberg. Far too many people have lost faith in the FBI, and I understand why completely. It doesn't help that some retired (and active) agents think what has happened over the last few years was appropriate. Their hate of President Trump is greater than their love of their country and the reputation of the FBI.

I can't change anyone's mind by saying this is abnormal behavior and the vast majority of FBI agents are good people who are just as shocked and dismayed as the American public. All I ask is for people to have an open mind and assign blame where blame is warranted.

The FBI has had its share of bad actors, and I hope they will be dealt with in the courts. But I don't know if that will happen. If it doesn't, then we know the justice system is gone and won't be coming back any time soon. I hope I am wrong.

I hope this book will help you on your journey, whatever that may be.

Use this information wisely to protect you and yours.

Frank L. Runles

Fredericksburg, VA

October 1, 2021

NOTES

INTRODUCTION

1. Adam S. H. & Jarvis J.P. (2006). Indicators of Veracity and Deception: An analysis of written statements made to police., Speech, Language and Law, 13, 1-22

2. Burgoon J.K. & Qin, T. (2006). The Dynamic nature of Deceptive Verbal Communication., Journal of Language and Social Psychology, 25, 76-96

3. Porter S. & Yuille J.C. (1996). The Language of Deceit: An Investigation of the Verbal Clues rot Deception in the Interrogation Context., Law and Human Behavior, 20, 443 - 458

CHAPTER 1: Deceptive Language Analysis

1. Joe Navarro, (July 2018). "The End of Deception", Psychology Today.

2. Timothy R. Levine (2020). "Duped: Truth-Default Theory and the Social Science of Lying and Deception", Tuscaloosa, AL, University of Alabama Press

CHAPTER 2: Listening with Curiosity

1. Goleman, Daniel (1995). Emotional Intelligence, New York, New York, Bantam Books.

2. Kahnaman, Daniel (2011). Thinking, Fast and Slow, New York, New York, Farrar, Straus & Giroux

3. Voss, Chris, & Raz, Tahl (2016). Never Split the Difference: Negotiating as if your life depends on it. London, Great Britain, Random House Business Books

CHAPTER 3: Balanced vs. Unbalanced Statements

1. Rabon, Don (2012). Investigative Discourse Analysis, Durham, NC, Carolina Academic Press

2. Rudacille, Wendell (1994). Identifying lies in disguise, Dubuque, IA, Kendall/Hunt Publishing Co.

Chapter 4: Indicators of Veracity

1. M.K. Johnson, M.A. Foley, A.G. Suengas, & C.L. Raye; "Phenomenal characteristics of memories for perceived & imagined autobiographical events." Journal of Experimental Psychology: General, Vol 117 (4), Dec 1988, 371-376

2. John Medina, (2008). Brain Rules, Seattle, WA, Pear Press.

3. Baddeley, A.D., & Hitch, G. (1974). Working memory. In G.H. Bower (Ed.), The psychology of learning and motivation: Advances in research and theory (Vol. 8, pp. 47--89). New York: Academic Press.

4. Adam S. H. & Jarvis J.P. (2006). Indicators of Veracity and Deception: An analysis of written statements made to police., Speech, Language and Law, 13, 1-22.

CHAPTER 5: Emotions

1. Emotions Revealed: Recognizing Faces and Feelings to Improve Communications and Emotional Life"

2. M.K. Johnson, M.A. Foley, A.G. Suengas, & C.L. Raye, (1988). "Phenomenal characteristics of memories for perceived and imaged autobiographical events", Journal of Experimental Psychology, 117(4)

CHAPTER 9: Cast of Characters and Nouns

1. Seth Stephen Davidowitz. (2017). Everybody Lies: Big Data, New Data, and What the Internet Can Tell Us About Who We Really Are", New York, New York, Dey Street, an HarperCollins imprint.